BLOOD
ON THE
TRACKS

BLOOD
ON THE
TRACKS

A History of
Railway
Crime
in Britain

David Brandon and Alan Brooke

First published 2010
This paperback edition published 2017

The History Press
The Mill, Brimscombe Port
Stroud, Gloucestershire, GL5 2QG
www.thehistorypress.co.uk

© David Brandon & Alan Brooke, 2010, 2017

The rights of David Brandon & Alan Brooke to be identified as the
Authors of this work has been asserted in accordance with the
Copyright, Designs and Patents Act 1988.

British Library Cataloguing in Publication Data.
A catalogue record for this book is available from the British Library.

ISBN 978 0 7509 8269 6

Typesetting and origination by The History Press
Printed and bound by CPI Group (UK) Ltd

CONTENTS

Stockport Viaduct. This view gives some idea how the viaduct over the Mersey Valley dominates the centre of Stockport.

INTRODUCTION

Communication is a necessity for civilised societies. The earliest such societies were located in the valleys of great rivers such as the Nile and the Indus. The water of the rivers provided the means for irrigation and thereby the development of agriculture; they also provided the means of transport and communication for these early civilizations. The inhabitants of these societies learned how to use draught animals for agricultural purposes. However, they found what they had developed was threatened by barbarian enemies who, while not so advanced economically, had utilised the horse for the purposes of transport and particularly for warfare.

The speed of the horse, its relative intelligence and the ways in which it could be trained gave those who exploited it a huge advantage. It would not be unfair to say that, for a millennium and more, the horse was the key to economic, military and political power. The problem with the horse was the finite limits on its capacity and endurance. A horse could only go so fast, or a team of horses could only pull so heavy a load, or go at such a speed. A messenger could ride no faster from, say London to York in 1700, than his predecessor would have done in 1200. By the late eighteenth century, the then advanced world needed a new, more efficient and more powerful horse. This could only be a mechanical horse or, in that happy transatlantic phrase, an 'Iron Horse'.

The invention of such a device was both a product of, and also a vital contributor to, that extraordinarily complex series of interacting processes which historians loosely – but conveniently – call the Industrial Revolution. This involved massive increases in humankind's control over nature, in the output and productivity of human labour and the scale and complexity of human co-operation and social organisation. The Industrial Revolution set in motion many of the economic and social processes which characterise the modern world, not least the expectation in the advanced economies that citizens have the right to enjoy a more or less continuous rise in their living standards and expectations.

The Industrial Revolution and associated technical and scientific developments in agriculture, as well as changes in landownership, meant that a hugely increased and predominantly urban population was supplied with food by a drastically reduced rural workforce. Those innumerable small towns and villages, each a centre of its immediate economic hinterland, that had been so characteristic of pre-industrial Britain, either stagnated or grew and transformed into centres of industry.

In the towns a radically new social fabric developed. Long-established social inter-relationships were destroyed. For example, the old semi-paternal nexus between squire and tenant, tenant farmer and labourer, priest and congregation, master and servant became anachronisms. Society was dominated by less personal relationships, such as those of employer and employee and producer and consumer. Most of all, the Industrial Revolution saw the emergence of the modern working class or proletariat; workers who sold their labour-power in exchange for wages, sometimes being employed in workforces of hundreds or thousands in factories and mills.

In finding their needs totally at odds with those of their employers, they learned from experience that the only way to defend and develop their interests was by collective industrial action. Workers' self-help, especially in the form of trade unions, gave expression to this. The bringing together of huge numbers of impoverished or poor people in the industrial towns created public health, public order and other issues which could only be addressed by radical changes in social policy. With the improvement in communications and the overall rise in real wages, production increasingly was for national but also international markets. The British economy became embroiled in a tangle of worldwide commercial and financial business transactions: it was the beginning of globalisation.

All this amounted to a revolutionary change in almost every aspect of life. Although some parts of the process can be seen to have started developing momentum as far as back as the sixteenth and seventeenth centuries, it was in the eighteenth and especially the nineteenth centuries that the processes matured. If just one factor had to be identified as critical to industrialisation and all its associated changes, it would have to be the invention of reasonably efficient steam engines.

They provided the power for mechanised forms of industrial production and, after much further trial and error, were a prime mover in the field of transport. The latter was, of course, the steam locomotive. The quite extraordinary rise of the railways in the nineteenth century was an effect of industrialisation and its associated changes, but it was also the cause of further massive economic, social and political change. In the words of Professor Harold Perkin, 'The Industrial Revolution's most spectacular achievement [was]: the development of the steam railway.'[1]

It is hard for us in the twenty-first century to appreciate the extent to which railways dominated land transport by the end of the nineteenth century. The statistics of their achievement are impressive. Between 1840 and 1870, annual passenger numbers rose from around 20 million to 336 million, and the amount of freight moved from 5 million to almost 170 million tons. Scarcely any town of any size was not served by one or more railway lines by 1900. The few towns that were never linked to the network either stagnated or actually declined even during the periods of sustained economic growth that made up much of the second half of the nineteenth century.

The railways also had a massive social, economic, intellectual and cultural impact. Processes of change from within and without are the dynamic of any society. The speed of change in Britain was enormously enhanced by the development of the railways. While some significant improvement to internal transport had been effected by turnpike roads and by canals, it was the railways that effectively 'shrank' the British Isles, and made that which was previously distant, close. The first simple lines usually connected quarries and mines to the nearest navigable waterway, and little interest was expressed in the conveyance of passengers. The success of the Liverpool & Manchester Railway in 1830 in benefiting the business communities of those cities was compounded when, to everyone's surprise, it was found that there was also a demand for passenger travel, much of it just for pleasure.

The coming of the railways meant that a reasonably cheap form of transport was available throughout the land for moving minerals, raw materials and the products of industry. That was their prime purpose. The growth of significant business in moving people had not been foreseen and was a bonus. The very idea that people would travel in large numbers for pleasure would have seemed utterly ludicrous in 1700 when travel was relatively and absolutely slow, expensive, difficult and often dangerous. Within the next 150 years, however, large numbers of people, excluding all but the very poorest sections of society, were benefiting from the enormous broadening of horizons that much easier and cheaper travel brought.

The railways contributed enormously to economic and social change. They broke down rural isolation, they enabled labour and capital to be much more flexible and mobile, all factors essential for a modern industrialising economy, and they were part of the process of eroding family, local, district and national identities within Greater Britain. Railways undermined existing social and cultural practices. They greatly increased the speed with which ideas and information could be transmitted, and assisted the spread of the written word and of reading as an activity both with serious purposes in mind and just for simple pleasure.

From the early days of the railways, the idea spread that actually sitting in a carriage during a journey was intrinsically boring and that something needed to be bought in order to help while away the time. Bookstalls appeared, selling newspapers, magazines and cheap novels, and this material was consumed in almost exponentially increasing amounts as the century wore on. Those who considered themselves a cut above the common herd, however, deplored the quality of this popular printed matter. It was cheap, sensational and vulgar, they said.

Millions used the railways to travel to the Great Exhibition held in Hyde Park in London in 1851. This glorified international trade fair was believed by its organisers to be an aid to international amity through the forging of trading and other commercial links between countries across the world. It was also designed to be a shop window to show off the multifarious achievements of British industry. Not without good reason was Britain being described at the time as 'the workshop of the world'.

The Exhibition was open from May to October 1851 and it contained 13,000 exhibits and was visited by 6.2 million people. The railways brought them from the four corners of the British Isles, largely in special trains at incredibly cheap prices. Many of these British visitors had rarely left the districts in which they were born, and the very idea of a visit to London, let alone a tour of such an Exhibition housed in a building which itself was the product of the latest technology, would have been something simply inconceivable for earlier generations. They were awed, educated and entertained by what they saw – a hugely mind-broadening experience. The Great Exhibition, a symbol that Britain was about to enter its historically brief period of world domination, was also a symbol of the contribution made by the railways to economic and social advancement.

While there were aspects of the railways that could be described as demotic, for example the way they allowed people from all walks of life and all parts of the country the chance of a cheap visit to the Great Exhibition, elsewhere railways emphasised social classes and gradations. A journey by rail was likely to provide stark evidence of how the well-to-do could afford to live in far more pleasant surroundings than many of the industrial workers who often had little choice but to dwell cheek by jowl with the noxious and polluting mines, mills, foundries and other workplaces in which they were employed. This starkly brought the observer face to face with the reality of the 'two nations' idea that exercised the conscience of many upper-class Victorians.

The comfort and service provided for the traveller by the railway companies varied greatly with the price he or she was prepared to pay. Accommodation

The Crystal Palace in Hyde Park, housing the Great Exhibition of 1851. The exhibition owed much of its great success to the railways who provided cheap inclusive fares to make it possible for people from right across Britain to visit it, many of them making their first trip ever to London. For some, it was the first time they had been away from home.

on trains was strictly divided in the early days into first, second, third and, in one or two cases, even fourth class. This segregation was repeated in station facilities such as waiting rooms, leading to immortal messages in frosted-glass windows such as 'third-class women's waiting room.'

The larger railway companies were among the very biggest capitalist business concerns of their time. In that sense, they provided a forerunner to the immense multi-national companies that bestride the globe in the twenty-first century. They were bang up to date in that the ownership, which was mostly in the hands of shareholders, was divorced from the everyday control which was exercised by professional managers – another feature of modern capitalism. These people were the top dogs in the railway employees' very hierarchical structure.

Some historians have even seen elements of feudalism in the way in which these companies organised their labour forces. Everyone knew their place within the scheme of things but realistically that is where the parallels with feudal society ended. A railway worker who kept a clean disciplinary record had a job for life if he wanted it. He had the possibility of promotion and employment with some social status attached to it, especially enjoyed by grades such as locomotive drivers and firemen. However, wages and conditions were often extremely poor and hours were long, even by the standards of the time.

The absolute priority given to safety issues was cited as the reason why there was a substantial degree of militarism present in the way in which railway companies organised their labour forces. A railway worker clocking on was 'reporting for duty'; the job he held was a 'post' at which he remained until relieved; and a worker liable to be disciplined might find himself 'on a charge.' The need for operational safety and the sheer scale of their operations required the maintenance of comprehensive and meticulous paper records, and for that reason the railway companies demanded a high level of literacy from its work-force and encouraged them to take their education further. However, the first major trade union in the industry had the revealing name of the 'Amalgamated Society of Railway Servants.' There was little that was paternalistic in the rela-tionship between the railway companies and their labour forces.

Railways from the start provoked deep anxieties and deep opposition. Many saw railways as essentially unnatural, as being by their very nature inim-ical to established ways of doing things, but also harmful to human minds and bodies. Trains, it was claimed, would damage crops and prevent hens laying their eggs, they would suffocate people travelling through tunnels, or, equally, the tunnels themselves would collapse pulverising the luckless passengers. Hundreds would die as the result of boiler explosions or as trains hurtled off the tracks and plunged over the edge of viaducts.

From another angle, it was averred that the lower orders would become fractious and discontented by being able to travel around. John Ruskin, vigor-ously attempting to keep railways out of his beloved Lake District, predicted 'the certainty…of the deterioration of moral character in the inhabitants of every district penetrated by the railway.' Mind you, when we read that Ruskin on his wedding night was apparently so horrified by the unexpected sight of his wife's pubic hair that he could not consummate the marriage, it becomes difficult to take anything he said very seriously.

The initial, almost primeval, fears and neuroses stirred up by the railways gradually changed their nature over the course of the nineteenth century, as even those who opposed them realised that the railways were here to stay. As they developed, they became an ever more potent symbol of modernity and the threats that modernity posed. The scale and complexity of their operations, the sublime nature of their major engineering feats (think, for example, of Stockport Viaduct dominating the town and the valley of the River Mersey), the manifest power and speed of the locomotives – all these had the power both to fascinate and to appal.

The railways seemed to encapsulate the forces of mechanisation, of organi-sation and industrial progress that were the very essence of emerging modern civilization. For good and for bad, or so it was seen at the time.

For many there was evil in this emerging new world, and the railways provided abundant evidence of it. Railways conveyed passengers at previously undreamed of speeds. Those people were, at least in the early days, trapped in small wooden boxes which shook them about, assaulted their senses and rendered them completely at the mercy of forces over which they themselves had no control. One critic described a railway traveller as a 'living parcel', merely being consigned or sent from one place to another.

The railways intruded into the environment. Their smoke, their whistles, the puffing of their locomotives, the clanging of buffers and the squeal of wheel flanges – all these created an appalling and unacceptable cacophony. Whole districts were demolished for their stations, sidings, sheds and marshalling yards. The verdant countryside was torn up to allow the passage of the iron horse and the tracks, without which they could not move. Tunnels burrowed under mountains, the cuttings and embankments changed the changelessness of the British countryside forever, and lofty viaducts reared up over valleys overawing the mere people who lived and worked below. Even time was hijacked. Gone were the one-handed clocks of the past to be replaced by railway time across the whole country, and a plethora of timetables, instructions and regulations. Man had created this beast; man was in danger of being taken over by it.

While the railways required order and discipline in their employees, and indeed in their passengers, railway installations and especially stations from the start attracted all manner of human detritus, not least that element bent on criminal enterprise. Particularly in those happy days when even small wayside stations had waiting rooms with roaring fires on cold winter days, stations could provide warmth and shelter. Many of today's unmanned stations offer cold comfort – even for paying passengers. A bus shelter on a railway platform is an admission of bad faith.

However, the large stations of the past could almost have been designed with society's drifters in mind. Some provided open access to covered space twenty-four hours a day. That had to be much better than dossing under the stars in sub-zero temperatures. No wonder that, whether big or small, railway stations over the best part of 200 years have been gratefully utilised by the homeless and the friendless in order to snatch an hour or two of sleep or shelter.

Major railway stations such as big city termini have also attracted a diverse stream of people operating just inside, or often most definitely outside, the law. Those offering freelance but illicit porterage services, for example female prostitutes and rent boys; procurers and procuresses; touts of all sorts; robbers; cadgers; those bent on sexual assault eying up their potential victims; cowboy taxi operators; con men looking for gullible marks; rich men, poor men, beggar men and thieves.

Big cities, especially London, have long attracted inward migration from the provinces. In many cases those who have been drawn to London have been bright, resourceful and energetic people, often young, who have found multifarious rewarding opportunities in the maelstrom of economic, commercial, cultural and other activities which is the life of the capital. For them the streets may not have exactly been paved with gold but they certainly brought them good fortune.

Another layer of incomers were those with skills that maybe attracted less remuneration, who perhaps left the provinces because of a shortage of economic opportunities. Substantial numbers of unemployed miners left South Wales in the depression of the 1930s and moved to London, in many cases to become milkmen. London offered them a better future. The size of London, the wealth generated there, its anonymity and the opportunities it offered for crime have attracted 'career criminals', many of whom have found rich pickings.

Unfortunately London has also always attracted the vulnerable and dysfunctional. For example, young people perhaps trying to get away from physical or other types of abuse at home; the bored and disaffected; drug addicts; people trying to escape from something (they do not necessarily know what); those restlessly seeking adventure or hoping that life in 'The Smoke' will kick-start their dreary lives. The best that many of them could look forward to is a succession of low-paid and menial jobs while living in squalid accommodation. They might be just as well off had they stayed in the surroundings that they knew and could deal with. Many of these drifters have certainly not been well equipped to deal with the dangers and temptations offered by the metropolis. Many were, and still are, lured into the sex trade.

This hotchpotch of humanity has tended to arrive by train, especially at King's Cross and Euston stations, evidence that many have come down from the north of England and from Scotland. The problems facing such new arrivals were dealt with by Michael Deakin and John Willis in a riveting but disturbing television documentary made in the 1970s and followed up by the book *Johnny Go Home*. They featured scared, callow, lonely and vulnerable arrivals, some of them literally children, and the reception committee of predatory low-life characters apparently ready to 'befriend' them as soon as they got off the train. The Transport Police know what goes on and can keep this activity under some degree of control but they cannot prevent it. It is almost as old as humanity itself, and it is certainly as old as London.

As a boy, one of the authors ranged far and wide throughout Britain in the quest to underline every engine number in his Ian Allan *ABC*. He did pretty well in that self-appointed task but fortunately his interest did not end there. Even at the age of twelve or thirteen as he travelled around, frequently absenting himself from school in order to do so, he began to ask questions which seemed to flow naturally from these trips.

Why might March, a small Fenland town in Cambridgeshire, have what some said were the largest railway marshalling yards in Western Europe? Why did some small settlements, no more than villages, have two or more railway stations? Why

The man for whom £2 was a small price to pay for the pleasure of smoking a pipe.

was there no major railway station in what could reasonably be described as central London? Why was it that Manchester, a large provincial city, had four major railway termini, all of which were on the periphery and most definitely not in the centre of the city? Why was Bristol's main station called 'Temple Meads' when there was not a blade of grass in sight? And why was it Carlisle 'Citadel' or Hull 'Paragon? Was the latter such a brilliant station? Who was the 'Doctor Day' of Doctor Day's Bridge Junction Signal Box just outside Bristol? He wanted to know the answers to these, and a thousand other, questions.

As he continued travelling around, and additionally began reading books about railways, he became aware of aspects of economic history, economic geography, topography and local history. He became fascinated by major (and minor) civil engineering features such as viaducts and tunnels, bridges, stations and hotels. Why were the mouths of some railway tunnels given features reminiscent of medieval castles? Why did some stations have what he came to know as Tudor or Jacobean or Gothic architectural motifs? He became aware of geological factors in the location of railway lines and other installations, and also in terms of regional building styles and building materials.

Regional and local cultural differences impinged on his awareness – most starkly at Newcastle Central when he asked another spotter if he knew the identity of a Gresley A4 Pacific puffing away into the distance. The answer provided by the friendly native was so unintelligible that it might as well have been uttered in Swahili. It was the future author's first brush with the Geordie accent. Via the medium of locomotive names, in particular those of the LMSR 'Jubilee' Class, he became aware of many obscure and far-flung parts of the former British Empire such as Bhopal, Bechuanaland and the Gilbert & Ellice Islands. He found out about great British sea dogs including Cornwallis, Barham and Tyrwhitt and battles such as Camperdown, Aboukir and Barfleur. Lastly, from the same class he was able to widen his vocabulary with the names of warships such as *Indomitable, Impregnable* and *Implacable*. Not bad for a class of 191 locomotives! A sense of curiosity and of needing to find out was stimulated. Fortunately this has continued and has made for a very interesting life.

This book brings together the authors' interest in social history and the history of crime, both subjects on which they have a number of published titles to their credit, with their enthusiasm for, and knowledge of, Britain's railways. They are particularly interested in the economic, social, political and cultural impact of the railways. This book is aimed at the general reader. It is necessarily selective and does not pretend to provide a comprehensive coverage of every type of crime committed on or around Britain's railways.

---

1   Perkin, H. *The Age of the Railway*, 1971.

CHAPTER ONE

ASSAULTS AND ROBBERIES

One early and enthusiastic historian of railways commented in 1851 that it was invariably safer to travel on the railway than to stay at home. Many of his contemporaries during the early years of the railways would not have agreed. Derailments, crashes and boiler explosions, for example, were unlikely to occur in the majority of homes, but were disconcertingly common experiences for railway travellers. So were spats with other travellers, as we shall see.

Travellers could rarely choose their fellow passengers. Antisocial behaviour resulting from overindulgence in alcohol led to many unsavoury scenes. Not the least of these occurred when men, with bladders clamouring for relief, exposed the necessary part of their anatomy in order to urinate out of moving trains. If the train was proceeding at speed, it was not unknown for passengers in carriages further down the train to find themselves subjected to a random shower of urine.

Many early railway carriages were, of course, open to the elements. Women especially, but also other men, could easily misconstrue the intentions of male travellers who started groping around in their nether regions in order to locate and extract their genitalia. Even this action, when intended for no more sinister a purpose than as the prelude to relieving themselves, was of course an infringement of public decency. A drunkard with a full bladder who was also believed to be a flasher or sex fiend really did not have a leg to stand on.

Many early passenger carriages contained a number of compartments, and the existence of this type of accommodation posed a whole world of problems for the sensitive traveller. The nature of the compartment meant that passengers were, by necessity, somewhat thrown together. In a crowded carriage there could be the most frightful situation of enforced physical intimacy, though those of a nervous disposition often found this easier to handle than the occupation of a compartment with just one fellow passenger. This stranger might turn out to be a robber, a sexual predator with curious or repulsive preferences, a homicidal maniac, a lunatic, a chain-smoker or a mind-numbingly tedious bore.

Robberies and assaults within the confinement of compartments were by no means uncommon. People felt trapped inside these small spaces, and although the vast majority of such journeys were completed without anything untoward happening, the reality that there was no easy way to stop the train, or even to contact a member of its crew, was a threatening one. Travellers therefore sometimes equipped themselves with weapons up to and including firearms before they embarked on train journeys. A traveller in 1854 admitted in a letter to a local newspaper that he never travelled by train without a loaded revolver in case he found himself tête-à-tête in an otherwise empty compartment with a lunatic or dangerous criminal on the run.

Before the days of lighting on trains, it was generally felt that tunnels were the places where assaults were most likely to happen. Advice to those alone in a compartment with only one other traveller was to be prepared for an attack by placing the hands and arms in the fashion best suited for defence. Ladies often had a hat pin at the ready. It was always felt that female travellers were more vulnerable to the various hazards of early train travel, especially those involving sexual or other forms of assault. For this reason some compartments were designated 'Ladies Only'. Of course simply labelling a compartment for the use of women only did not prevent some determined male reprobate from jumping in when the guard's back was turned. In Victorian melodramas the blackguard concerned would invariably proceed to subject his female victim to a fate worse than death.

Even railway employees were not above taking advantage of female travellers on their own. A guard of what later became the London, Brighton & South Coast Railway was dismissed in 1841 after he had very solicitously suggested to a female passenger that she move from one compartment to another which was more comfortable and reserved for ladies. He carried her bag for her, but then remained in the compartment when the train started and attempted to take what were coyly described as 'certain liberties' with her. She fought back, preserving her virtue, only to be ungraciously thrown out by the guard onto the platform of the next station at which the train stopped.

Many other horrors could await the female traveller in 'Ladies Only' compartments. She might have to put up with screaming or otherwise fractious mothers, children and/or babies, mothers breastfeeding (which was frowned upon by those who considered themselves genteel), women beggars and others with sob stories they needed to get off their chests. It was by no

MAKING THE BEST OF IT.

First Passenger (horrified at seeing the other burst into the carriage while the train was in motion).—GOODNESS, MAN, YOU'VE HAD A NARROW ESCAPE !

Second Passenger.—I HAVE. THERE WAS A SOLITARY LADY IN THE COMPARTMENT I SCRAMBLED OUT OF.

Making the Best of It.

means unknown for prostitutes to ply their trade, particularly in otherwise empty 'Ladies Only' compartments. The especially determined ones thought nothing of ejecting a single female occupant and replacing her with the client of the moment. Ideally the trains involved in these activities were not stopping-at-all-stations trains on busy inner-city or suburban routes. 'Ladies Only' compartments finally disappeared in the 1970s.

It was not unknown for men travelling in a compartment with just an unknown woman for company to find themselves on the other end of a 'fate worse then death' situation. For reasons best known to themselves women passengers sometimes maliciously concocted stories that the men concerned had made indecent comments or suggestions, or had molested or sexually assaulted them. If there were no witnesses, the man, even if he was totally innocent, might find that his guilt was almost taken for granted, and he could very well find himself undertaking a lengthy and very uncongenial prison sentence.

Over the years small numbers of men had found themselves being black-mailed by women who pretended they had been assaulted and threatened to inform the authorities unless the man concerned parted with money. A woman who had shared a compartment with a male dentist on a train from Watford Junction to London Euston alleged that he had indecently assaulted her. She unwisely informed the court that the dastardly fellow had smoked a pipe throughout the entire journey. The court rejected her evidence on the basis that pipe-smoking and sexual assault were two activities which could not be carried out at the same time. It did not help her case that neither her body nor her clothes had borne any evidence that an assault had been made. However, it is no wonder that some men studiously avoided entering a com-partment containing a lone female traveller, just as some other men with evil intentions would have made a beeline for one. Over the years a number of women prostitutes did time for demanding money with menaces from lone male passengers on trains.

In 1875 one of the greatest sexual scandals of the nineteenth century hit the headlines. The British public has a keen and constantly salacious appetite for sex scandals, especially if they involve members of the social elite. The main player was Colonel Valentine Baker (1827-87), a well-respected and eminent professional soldier. He was forty-four years of age at the time. At Liphook in Hampshire Baker entered a first-class compartment of a train of the London & South Western Railway. It contained only one other passenger – a young woman called Kate Dickinson. She was attractive and from a well-connected and wealthy family. Perhaps unwisely, Baker engaged Kate in conversation.

As the train headed for London someone on the platform at Woking noted a young woman apparently hanging out of a carriage door. He notified the sta-tion staff and the train was stopped near Esher. Kate informed the police that Baker had 'insulted' her, a euphemism for sexual assault. Baker had to attend court to face a charge of 'assault with attempt to ravish'. The scandal-mongers of the gutter press got to work with relish, unearthing real information and inventing imaginary stories as necessary, and publishing them to an extent that prejudiced Baker having a fair trial.

Unsubstantiated rumours circulated to the effect that this was not the first time that he had been implicated in this kind of thing. The papers made much of the fact that Baker had a brother who had earlier caused a scandal of a dif-ferent sort when he married a young girl he had bought in a slave market, although this was hardly germane to the case under review. Baker was found guilty, but of assault rather than attempt to rape, sent to prison for a year, fined £500 and dismissed from the service. He spent much of his subsequent life

Valentine Baker, who was forced into exile after the incident on the train, but who went on to rebuild a successful career for himself overseas.

gaining fame and honours as a mercenary soldier but he was never rehabilitated by society. Some people thought that the relative leniency of the law in dealing with him was evidence of the class bias of the courts towards those in 'high places'.

Only members of the cloth seem to have been able to come through a compromising situation on the basis of their innocence generally being presumed. We shall never know exactly what was said or what went on when a young curate entered a compartment containing just a sixteen-year-old girl on a train of the Great Western Railway. The girl alleged that he had pulled her onto his knee, kissed her swan-like neck and whispered various intimate observations and suggestions into her ear.

The case went to court but the curate rejected all suggestions of wrong-doing on his part. He did admit that he had entered into conversation with the girl and had suggested that he might be able to get her a job playing the organ in his parish church. It was a most magnificent organ, he had boasted. Could this innocent comment have been taken as meaning something else? The court did not think so and the curate returned to his parish with his reputation unsullied.

In 1864 a gentleman sitting happily in the compartment of a London & South Western Railway train travelling between Surbiton and Woking was startled out of his ruminations when he found himself staring into a woman's face a few inches from his, looking in from the outside of the rapidly moving train. He leapt to help what clearly was a maiden in distress. She was stand-ing on the footboard of the carriage and clinging on for dear life, clothes and hair streaming in the wind. It was no easy matter to haul her to safety but fortunately some people by the side of the line spotted her predicament and alerted the guard who quickly brought the train to a halt.

A dastardly character by the name of Nash had earlier specifically selected and entered a compartment containing two female passengers, one of whom of course was our woman on the footboard, Mary Moody. Nash had attempted, with a marked lack of subtlety, to chat up the other woman but she had alighted at Surbiton. When this happened, Mary also tried to leave the carriage but she was a few seconds too late, and as the train steamed out on its way to Woking she found herself alone with the singularly unsavoury Nash.

He began to ask her a string of questions full of sexual innuendo. Maybe Mary's silence inflamed his passion because he first embraced her and then attempted to assault her indecently. That was when Mary saw little option but to attempt to escape his clutches via the compartment door and the carriage footboard. Nash was arrested and was hauled up in front of the magistrates.

In 1892 Mrs Mary Siddals, an attractive mother-of-two, was the victim of a serious sexual assault on a Midland Railway train travelling between Burton-on-Trent and Tamworth. She was alone in the compartment except for a man dressed in black who, having attacked her, tried to throw her out of the moving carriage. She was able to cling on for a few seconds but eventually fell off and tumbled down to the bottom of an embankment, receiving serious injuries.

A man was arrested and charged with assault and grievous bodily harm. His rather feeble defence was that Mary had been hallucinating. Two other witnesses came forward who attested that the man in black had made similar attacks on them. His work as a preacher and teacher of the young cut no ice with the court, and he was described as a 'sanctimonious hypocrite' before being sentenced to two years' hard labour, which most people thought was overly lenient.

Not all cases of sexual assault turned out to be that. A man entered a com-partment on a train of the North Eastern Railway near Durham. The only other passenger was a plump and homely looking woman aged about forty who sat opposite him. The train was only just pulling out of the station when she suddenly jumped up and asked him what he meant by what he had just done. He protested that he had not done anything except sit and look out of the window. A few minutes later the same thing happened again. This sce-nario was re-enacted several more times before the train slowed for a station, by which time the man was convinced that his fellow traveller was totally mad and a public danger.

Artistic licence is liberally employed in this view of Peterborough from the south. Crossing the bridge over the River Nene is a train on the Great Northern Railway, while another train can be seen on the tracks of the London & Birmingham Railway's long cross-country line from Blisworth to Peterborough.

As the train pulled into the station the woman leant out of the window shouting to the guard. The racket she was creating attracted that august official and a knot of bystanders. She angrily accused the man of trying to pinch her legs. He vehemently denied such intent. The man was beginning to feel a horrible black hole opening up in front of him when the guard suddenly recalled that he had placed a basket under the seat on which the woman was sitting. She suddenly cried out that it had happened again! Everyone crowding around could see that it could not possibly have been the accused. The culprit of the assault was revealed as a rather irascible goose which was occupying the basket under the seat and venting its spleen in the only way possible – by lashing out with its beak!

Not long after the Muller case of 1864, a violent and deranged man joined passengers in a crowded train at King's Cross. He proceeded to subject his fellow travellers on the 110-minute non-stop journey to Peterborough to a catalogue of horrifying experiences stopping short, however, of murder. In their compartment these passengers were literally captives, totally unable to alert the train crew to the activities of the maniac in their midst.

Public concern about these and similar events led to the passing in 1868 of The Regulation of Railways Act. It required that all passenger trains travelling more than twenty miles without stopping must be equipped with a functioning system whereby passengers could communicate with 'the servants of the company in charge of the train.' The installation of such a system did not eliminate the possibility of attacks, but certainly helped to make passengers feel more secure.

By this time the railway was becoming a very safe medium of travel. Incidentally, the above act also brought in a penalty for misuse of the communication cord. This was fixed at a maximum of £5 and remained the same for around 100 years. In doing so it staunchly avoided inflationary trends in the economy, to the point where to be fined under the act could almost be described as being good value for money.

Passengers, being the quirky or sometimes stupid people they can be, sometimes misunderstood or misused the communication cord facility when there was nothing remotely approaching an emergency. Throughout the history of the railways there have been others for whom the very existence of the device and its ready accessibility was a source of wayward fascination. They obviously saw the cord as something of a challenge and many succumbed to its allure. They pulled it, they paid the penalty!

Before the passing of the 1868 Act, anyone finding themselves in a compartment on fire, where an assault or other crime was taking place, or where someone had been taken ill, was advised to tie a brightly coloured handkerchief to the end of a stick and wave it as far out of the carriage as was commensurate with safety. Hopefully this cunning ploy would catch the attention of one of the railwaymen on board who would assume that there was an emergency and therefore would stop the train.

Equally, the railwayman concerned might assume that the person waving the stick embellished with the hanky was simply using it to salute an acquaintance or relation by the side of the line, or just flourishing it out of a sense of joie de vivre. In such cases he might not stop the train. Of course he certainly would not stop the train if he had been looking in the opposite direction all the time.

Some interesting suggestions were put forward for ways in which beleaguered passengers might make their plight known to members of the train crew. One earnest correspondent of the *Morning Herald* newspaper advocated a device he thought would do the trick. The guard of the train should wear a belt round his waist. Attached to this would be a long chain passing through every carriage and anyone who wished to summon the assistance of the guard would be able to alert him by simply tugging the belt. Such a device was worthy of Heath Robinson at his very best.

Another suggestion, even more monstrously impractical, involved open parachutes above every carriage of a moving train. For any passenger needing to communicate urgently with the guard, it was simplicity itself. He or she merely tugged a string to close the parachute whereupon the lynx-eyed guard, having spotted the deflation, would bring the train to an immediate halt. Another ingenious solution involved a speaking tube running the length of the train. A passenger in dire straits would be able to summon instant succour simply by speaking into the mouthpiece. So long, presumably, that the guard did not have his attention distracted by any of the thousand and one other duties his post entailed.

A professional railwayman who fancied himself as a serious, even groundbreaking, inventor, gave a public demonstration of an electrical apparatus which would set a bell ringing on the footplate when activated by a passenger needing assistance. He spent twenty minutes or so explaining the principles of physics that were involved in this cunning device. In doing this he bored his audience to the verge of insensibility but they perked up considerably when with a flourish he announced that he was now going to dazzle them by a demonstration of the capabilities of his failsafe apparatus.

Failsafe it may have been, foolproof it was not! The proud inventor, who became increasingly flustered and pompous, tried again and again without success to elicit a response from his brainchild against the background of a rising crescendo of ribald and unhelpful comments from his uncharitable audience. Eventually they made their way home, still holding their sides with painful and uncontrollable mirth. For them the demonstration had been a huge success.

In 1884 Captain John Preston of the Berkshire Militia, accompanied by his wife, entered a second-class compartment in a Great Western train. They joined it at Paddington. Its destination was Oxford. Two ladies already occupied the carriage. They were Mrs Frances de Windt and her sister, Miss Margaret Long. Mrs de Windt promptly informed them that the compartment was reserved for some friends she was expecting. Preston then told Mrs de Windt that the guard had pointed them to this particular compartment. Mrs de Windt then commented that this was just the sort of incident that occurred when one travelled with one's social inferiors. Her next pronouncement was that she would have the guard dismissed. These kind words thankfully fell on deaf ears and Preston and his wife then attempted to sit down.

This was difficult because the original occupants of the compartment had randomly scattered a large and antediluvian collection of parcels all over the seats. They made no attempt to move these and so the good captain and his wife had to make the best of a bad job and sit, uncomfortably, where they could. When Preston ventured to place one of the parcels on the floor Mrs de Windt flew into a tantrum, asked him for his name and said that her husband would be calling on him the next day. He refused to give his name.

The journey continued in uneasy silence until the first stop at Reading where Mrs de Windt summoned the guard. She told him that the captain had grossly insulted her and she loudly demanded to be assisted to another carriage. A crowd quickly gathered, avid for some free entertainment. They pricked up their ears when the words 'grossly insulted' were voiced. This was taken to suggest that the captain had uttered salacious words or acted in a lewd way towards Mrs de Windt.

Three days later Mr de Windt and a friend called Russell who was a retired army officer, arrived at Captain Preston's home in Abingdon and handed him a note. It demanded an apology for his insulting behaviour towards Mrs de Windt on the train three days earlier. It questioned whether Captain Preston, despite being an officer, could properly be described as a gentleman since by definition no gentleman would insult a lady.

When Captain Preston tried to give his side of the story and refused to apologise, de Windt called him a damned scoundrel and punched him on the shoulder. When he attempted to land another blow Preston parried it and gripped his hand tightly whereupon de Windt squealed with pain and, calling Preston a brute, told him that he had broken his finger. Clearly de Windt was beside himself with rage because he then spat out the words 'I wouldn't be seen with you at a pig fight, you white-livered scoundrel,' and added menacingly that he would see to it that Preston was blackballed by his club.

This instructive example of how certain members of the Victorian middle class exercised their interpersonal skills went to the courts for adjudication. Preston was vindicated because he was awarded £50 damages for assault. A counterclaim by de Windt for damages of £500 for his broken finger was contemptuously dismissed. It is obvious that oversensitivity and readiness to see insult ran in de Windt's family. His father had once fought a duel with a man who had made disparaging remarks about the necktie he was wearing.

Many courts had a considerable amount of their time taken up with cases of assault on the railways. The nature of these assaults was as varied as the people who committed them. What are we to make of the two students fined 30 shillings by Hammersmith magistrates for leaning over a division between two compartments and spitting onto the hat and a book belonging to a doctor?

At Southport the magistrates fined a solicitor aged seventy just 5 shillings when he ran out of patience and used his umbrella to show his displeasure and knock off the hat belonging to a man who, for two whole years, had refused to admit him into the compartment he habitually shared with two other men. They spent their journeys playing whist and they clearly thought this gave them exclusive rights to the occupancy of the compartment. Such a paltry fine suggests that the court sympathised with the aged but feisty solicitor.

It was possible to hire containers of hot coals for use as foot-warmers in unheated carriages on cold days. Fights were no means unknown when other passengers who could not, or would not, hire their own foot-warmers tried to place their feet so as to benefit from the heat generated by the foot-warmer hired by another passenger who had paid for the privilege. The latter would jealously guard their source of pedal comfort against others, using physical force if necessary. Passengers were earnestly encouraged not to engage in debates with strangers about religion or politics as a way of avoiding the likelihood of fisticuffs. That these contentious issues did frequently lead to disputes with violent outcomes is shown by the records of innumerable minor courts up and down the country.

Probably for every petty case of assault or fighting that went as far as the courts and was therefore recorded, there were innumerable others where the victims or participants did not have recourse to the law. Clearly these have mostly been forgotten, but one that is still remembered occurred when four burly farmers were joined in their compartment by a large and well-built man who proceeded, without obvious provocation, to insult and curse each of them in turn and in the most scurrilous fashion.

A request that he bridled his tongue evoked the man's wrath, and he proceeded to crank up both the sound volume and the vituperative nature of the comments he was making. Having given the man one final chance, which only unleashed a further torrent of abuse, the four farmers then waited for the next station and seized the man who they then proceeded to throw into a duck pond close by the side of the line. Serves him right.

Assault was not always intentional. A man had been attacked by footpads in the street near Willesden Junction but had scared them off when he took out his pistol and fired over their heads. So elated had he been by this robust defence of his own person and property that a few days later he was relating the event to a stranger on a train. He was warming to his theme and becoming highly excited, he decided to re-enact his reaction to the approach of the footpads. He took out his pistol and fired it. His aim was not as true as it should have been because instead of firing across his interlocutor's head, the bullet literally made a neat parting in the latter's hair!

An obstreperous Welsh collier attracted a short custodial sentence after he climbed out the carriage window of a compartment on a moving train on the Taff Vale Railway and rode on the roof for some distance. Clearly a man of some acrobatic ability, he then swung entirely unexpectedly through the open window of another compartment and proceeded to pull one passenger's hair and to punch another. Earlier in the same day he had managed to break a window and assault two railway officials at Aberdare station. After all this hyperactivity a couple of months cooling off in a cell hopefully gave him time to ponder on his foolishness.

Assaults by members of the railway staff on members of the public were by no means unknown. In 1839 a Great Western Railway employee, out of uniform, became involved in a fracas going on in a compartment where two passengers were disputing the right to sit in the same seat. The Great Western

Railwayman seems to have been overzealous and, seizing one of the passengers, deposited him in a heap on the platform, a piece of officiousness for which he was fined £25.

It is well known that little love was lost between rival railway companies, but this usually remained on a corporate rather than a personal basis. However, in 1843 the long-standing mutual loathing between the chairman of the London & Croydon Railway and a former director of two other companies had seen a scrimmage on a station, when one hit the other with a cane only to get a neat uppercut for his efforts. A duel was arranged, but these by now had become illegal, and the would-be contestants were prosecuted and bound over to keep the peace.

Ely is a small and quiet cathedral city but the tranquillity of the station was rudely shattered one day in 1847 when a male passenger made a maniacal attack on the other travellers in his compartment. He then hit the stationmaster and had to be locked up for the night. His defence was that he had a condition whereby he lost control of his actions after imbibing alcohol; on this occasion he had drunk one brandy. The court tended towards leniency and he was fined just £5!

Two respectable ladies were in a London, Brighton & South Coast train heading for London one day in 1904 when they were joined by a man who immediately leant out of the window, shouting and gesticulating. Then, so the ladies claimed, he took out a knife and lunged at one of them, unexpectedly and without provocation. Nothing daunted, one of the ladies grabbed the knife, passing it to her friend who threw it out of the window. Perhaps the man did not expect such a doughty response because he quickly found himself pinioned in a corner of the carriage until East Croydon, where the station officials were alerted and he was arrested. His defence that he had simply taken the knife out to trim his cigar was rejected and he was sentenced to hard labour.

Railways provided a host of new opportunities for Britain's criminal elements. The environs of stations, goods depots and marshalling yards provided a myriad of opportunities for theft and robbery. One type of robbery which did not necessarily involve violence was that usually employed by small syndicates who lured unwary or credulous passengers into card games or other games of chance. The usual procedure was for a group, usually of three or four men, to enter a railway compartment on a train going a considerable distance. They did this when they had espied one or more likely marks, but they took their place on the train as if they did not know each other.

A few minutes into the journey one of the men would take out a pack of cards and suggest a game or two to while away the time. His unacknowledged accomplices would agree and might then invite anyone else in the compart-

First Class

Second Class

Satirical depiction of the type of public behaviour expected from, respectively, first, second and third-class early railway passengers. In reality the biggest rogues were probably in the first class.

ment to join them. If this happened, then the stranger would be allowed some useful initial wins and, as his enthusiasm and greed grew, the stakes rose correspondingly. The card sharps, however, were often highly skilled at taking their victim along with them but the outcome was usually the same – the victim was fleeced, yet reluctant to inform friends or authority for fear of looking stupid.

The activities of these robbers of the iron road caused a newspaper correspondent to call for the return of Dick Turpin who he thought a capital and upright fellow compared to these devious cowards who infested Britain's railway carriages. Sometimes these crooks threatened their victims with a dusting-up if they did not join the card games.

Pickpockets found rich reward for their efforts in densely packed railway stations and within crowded carriages. In the latter a common ploy was for a pickpocket with charm and plausibility to express concern for a wealthy looking traveller and offer to swap seats, away from a draught, for example. The thief would have already noted the disposition of likely valuables about his victim's person, and in the minor melee created by changing seats in a crowded compartment would have deftly removed these items. We should not underestimate the skill required not only in taking the items without detection, but also in picking the right victim, obtaining agreement for the move, and for timing this just before a station stop where the pickpocket of course left the train and disappeared.

An investigator for *Tit-Bits* interviewed an instructor in the art of picking pockets who declared proudly that it was every bit 'as much a fine art as pianoforte-playing or high-class conjuring'. The experienced and successful thieves were members of the 'swell mob', prominent in the hierarchy of the criminal world, and always clean and respectably well dressed. Their resourcefulness and ingenuity could be quite extraordinary. Pickpockets, of course, still ply their trade on today's railways, crowded trains on the London Underground being a favoured hunting ground. They work in small groups, and the villain who actually does the stealing quickly and surreptitiously passes the items on to others in the syndicate. Few victims realise that they have been robbed until later, by which time they may be far from the scene.

Another different kind of villain was, and is, the luggage or baggage thief. The extent of their depredations is indicated by the fact that in the 1870s on the Eastern Counties Railway seventy-six passengers lost items of luggage in just one day. One of the most spectacular hauls made by such thieves occurred in the 1870s at Paddington station of the Great Western Railway. A member of the Countess of Dudley's entourage foolishly placed her employer's jewel box on the floor for a few seconds while helping a colleague. It vanished in a trice. The contents, which consisted of diamonds worth £50,000, were never recovered. Perhaps the offered reward of £1,000 was insufficient.

A drawing by the French artist Gustav Dore of a workman's train on the Metropolitan Railway. Probably few thieves and pickpockets would be at work at this time of day but crowded, ill-lit platforms on the early underground were a happy hunting ground for the light-fingered fraternity.

The thief who picked up a package from a Euston to Liverpool train in 1907 must have been well pleased when he found it contained 2,000 gold half-sovereigns. Determined thieves have found ways to break into left-luggage lockers and others have forged cloakroom tickets in order to claim deposited items belonging to other people.

Those who stole pieces of luggage can never have been absolutely certain what these would contain, and must occasionally have had red faces when the contents of the stolen items were revealed as worthless. Dirty washing being taken to the laundry was one such item. A man was convicted at Taunton in 1892 for stealing a valise. It contained travellers' samples of false teeth.

What about the man who illicitly took a station barrow to remove a heavy box, only to find when he had trundled it out the station environs that it contained turnips – nothing but turnips! This vegetable has never had much of a street value. However, the youth of fifteen who feloniously removed a hamper containing four dozen live rabbits found a ready market for them in the streets of Derby. The magistrates took a dim view of this enterprise and gave him two months of hard labour.

A busy period of comings and goings at a London station around 1840. It is easy to see how such apparent chaos provided golden opportunities for pickpockets and luggage thieves.

Unfortunately railway employees have, from time to time, succumbed to the temptation to pilfer luggage or goods in transit. A desperado by the name of Frost obtained a job as a passenger guard on the Great Western Railway, probably with theft in mind. Late in 1848 the Earl of Craven complained long and loudly about the disappearance of items of his luggage from Shrivenham station in Wiltshire. An investigation was set in motion which failed to recover the missing items or unearth any suspect. However, in 1849 Frost was discovered by a supervisor removing items of clothing from the luggage in his van. He leapt out of the slowly moving train but was arrested and charged with theft. He was carrying a pistol and he asked for other cases to be taken into consideration.

Items recorded as having been stolen by staff from parcels or luggage, on railway premises or on trains, have included cash, clothing, jewellery, gramophone records, footwear and even trunks and cases themselves, all of which might interest a receiver of stolen goods who would pay good prices for them. Sometimes items were taken which turned out to have little or no value on the black market. Sacked railway employees have found themselves doing time for having stolen, for example, travellers' samples, artists' materials, boxes of cricket balls, tins of paint, seedlings, doorknobs, geological specimens, rotting cheese and, perhaps best of all, baby alligators only a few inches long. It might have taken an effort to find a market for them.

Freight wagons standing in goods yards, sidings or marshalling yards could provide extremely tempting targets for the few bad eggs among the mass of railway workers. In 1889 eight men working for the Lancashire & Yorkshire Railway at Miles Platting, Manchester, filched a barrel of brandy and embarked on the drinking bout to end all such bouts. One of them died of alcohol poisoning but the others, being in advanced stages of inebriation, were unable to resist arrest. Still, they had had a great binge. For most of their existence the railways were common carriers, and the range of goods and merchandise they carried defied description. It was insider information that led to the theft of 800 Christmas puddings from Wellington Street goods depot, Leeds, in 1949. The railwaymen involved were caught and punished.

Those who say that crime does not pay certainly ought to get out more often. It would be more realistic to say that honesty does not pay as one passenger guard found out when in 1957 he found a handbag containing £3,829. He gave this in to a supervisor at what was then London Road station, Manchester. A passenger claimed the handbag and to show her gratitude she rewarded him with what used to be called half-a-crown. This generous gesture amounted to less than 0.1 per cent of the money in her handbag.

Most theft from the railways was carried out by members of the criminal fraternity, some merely opportunist, others well organised and planned. Excisable items like tobacco and spirits were among those of which the stealing needed most planning, but which also brought lucrative results.

Ironically the development of the internal combustion engine, the biggest threat to railway business, also assisted those wanting to steal from the railway. The massive growth in the number of small vans and cars in the 1950s and 1960s made it easy for such a vehicle to be driven into a goods yard, a sizeable and worthwhile quantity of goods to be taken and a quick getaway made.

A van was involved in a well-organised heist in July 1949. The thieves had obviously been watching train movements for some time and had established that an overnight freight from Nottingham to Darlington was usually put into the loop at Markham near Tuxford on the East Coast Main Line to allow faster trains to pass. A gang using a car drove into a field alongside the track and broke into the van containing cigarettes from Player's at Nottingham. They were seen, however, and rapidly apprehended. Over 170,000 cigarettes had been stolen and the gang members each received five years.

In 1954-5 another gang spent months visiting railway installations along the East Coast Main Line in Nottinghamshire, South Yorkshire and North Lincolnshire. This was the 'Margham Gang' named after its leader who had a well-known propensity for violence. They used a van and were successful for several months, getting away with wine, tea, tobacco and shoes, all of which would find a ready market. There was, however, an element of hit-and-miss in their operations and they seem to have been disgusted when they rifled a van containing carpets and textiles. These they left scattered around the scene of the crime. They cunningly varied their operations, keeping one jump ahead of the Transport Police, but were eventually caught after using extreme violence to resist arrest. Margham himself had the small matter of eighty-three previous convictions. Some might call him a career criminal.

In 1838 the railway companies were required by law to carry mails and post as directed by the postmaster general. Mail in transit provided a very tempting target for thieves. Some came to specialise in this type of crime and often did so with boldness and elan. One famous case occurred in 1849 on the Great Western Railway at Bridgewater where both the up and down overnight Exeter mail trains were robbed by the same gang.

The robbers, who were two fit and strong young men and needed to be, were in the carriage next to the van with mailbags on the up train. They opened the door of their compartment as the train was moving along rapidly, held on while clambering along the running board of their lurching carriage and then gained access to the mail van which was unattended. They concentrated on registered letters and other potentially valuable packets, which they stuffed into sacks they had brought along for precisely this purpose. When the train was slowing for its halt at Bristol, they dropped down to the track and made their way over a fence.

The robbery was quickly discovered but these two bold robbers returned a few hours later and performed the same operation on the down train. However, while they had been hanging around on Temple Meads station they had excited the suspicion of another man waiting for the same train. He gave the authorities a description and the robbers were quickly apprehended. They had almost certainly been responsible for a number of other robberies on the Great Western Railway.

The mails continued to be a tempting target for criminal activity right up to the loss of most rail-carried postal and mail traffic to air and the roads – itself, it could be said, a criminal waste of resources. Some of those who have robbed the mails have exercised great ingenuity. In the late 1960s one thief used to place himself in a large but light aluminium trunk. This desperado wore an oxygen mask in order to breathe and had himself delivered by accomplices to a busy station, hidden from sight in the trunk and signed for as a parcel. The trunk was then loaded into a train along with the mail bags.

He would listen and when he thought the coast was clear he would open the trunk, seize a few likely looking mailbags, pull them inside the trunk with him and then travel on with the train to wherever the trunk was due to be unloaded. There his accomplices would of course meet the trunk and carry it away,

William Tester   *Edward Agar*   *James Burgess*

Tester, Agar and Burgess who carried out the Great South Eastern Train Robbery.

opening it and examining the contents of the mail bags at their leisure. This criminal enterprise was successful for some time before he was caught, and it is thought that he had stolen something like £200,000 of valuables in this way.

Britain was shocked in 1855 by an extremely bold robbery on a moving train, the event quickly coming to be known as the 'Great South Eastern Bullion Robbery'. This was planned by two men. Edward Agar, an expert in the field of locks and as such highly regarded in the criminal underworld, and his accomplice, William Pierce, whose main motivation seems to have been hatred for the South Eastern Railway who had dismissed him in 1852. They recruited two workers employed by the South Eastern Railway: Burgess, a train guard, and Tester, a clerk whose duties included devising duty rosters for the company's guards.

They decided to rob a consignment of gold conveyed in a bullion van marshalled in a train from London to Folkestone. The problem was that the timing of the shipments was unpredictable. Each member of the gang had his assigned task. Tester's role was to ensure that Burgess was the guard when the next shipment was made, and he also copied keys for the safe carrying the gold. He had many dealings with the Chubb Company, makers of security locks. Agar and Pierce checked how the consignment was handled at the Folkestone end. The preparations were meticulous but also time-consuming because they involved watching the train every night. If Burgess gave the agreed signal, it indicated that the gold was aboard. Eventually their patience was rewarded, Burgess indicating that this was the night!

Agar and Pierce bought first-class tickets to Ostend via Dover and they took their seats in separate compartments. However, as arranged, Agar joined Burgess in the guard's van before the train started out. Agar got to work on the locks, and well before the train got to Folkestone the bags they had brought with them were filled with gold and the safe filled up with lead shot. Agar and Pierce returned to London on the first available train, the gold innocently carried in carpet bags. They then melted the gold down, the men already having a buyer, and the proceeds were then shared out as agreed. The total value was approaching £1 million by today's prices.

A great hue and cry went out when the robbery was discovered and the gang might well have got away with the whole thing had not Agar and Pierce fallen out. Agar had been sentenced to life imprisonment for another offence, uttering a forged cheque (he was possibly framed), and he eventually decided that he had nothing to lose by turning Queen's evidence which allowed him to drop Pierce in it, as they say. Pierce received only a two-year sentence but Tester and Burgess were transported to the Antipodes for fourteen years. They were viewed as particularly culpable because they had been employed in trusted positions by the South Eastern Railway.

The story of the Great Train Robbery has been told many times but it needs to be mentioned here, if only briefly. A number of thefts of mail from moving trains had been carried out by two gangs operating in the south of England in 1961 and 1962. They were not all particularly rewarding in terms of what they stole but the men gathered information about how the railway handled valuable consignments of mail, and in doing so learned that there were frequent shipments of untraceable bank notes from Scotland to London on an overnight train on the West Coast Main Line.

A criminal consortium was assembled to plan a robbery of this train. They included a self-taught expert in the science of tampering with signals and line-side electrical equipment. Several luminaries from the underworld made up this consortium which really was a gathering of all the relevant criminal talents. The outcome was a theft which netted over £2.5 million pounds. The robbery was planned with military precision and no small initial investment to 'buy' the right people for the various tasks involved in the project.

The robbery took place on 8 August 1963 near Cheddington in Buckinghamshire when the gang halted the southbound mail train at about three in the morning. Ironically, the gang were disappointed with their haul – they had been hoping for twice as much. One by one the gang members were arrested, convicted and sent to prison, mostly for extremely long terms, emphasising that this was officially seen as a crime against property, such crimes tending to be punished more harshly than crimes against the person.

The engine driver was very badly beaten after attempting to fight back and he received injuries which almost certainly shortened his life. Only a small amount of the stolen money was ever recovered and many people think that the robbery's chief organiser and investor, who received the largest share of the proceeds, was never identified and obviously never brought to justice.

Theft of railway property has been a constant problem from earliest times to the present. In the days when refreshment rooms and restaurant cars invariably used heavy-duty crockery, this disappeared in quite extraordinary quantities, as did cutlery. Light bulbs have always been a target of thieves and were stolen in large numbers, especially from carriages with closed compartments. The same type of compartment used to display the attractive publicity posters that older readers will remember. These were fixed above the seats and below the luggage racks and usually showed reproduction paintings or photographs of 'holiday haunts'.

Locals on a train travelling up the soot-laden steel-making district of the Don Valley out of Sheffield might be tempted to get away from it with a day out by train to sample the fleshpots of Cleethorpes or the boisterous delights of Blackpool. Elsewhere other passengers travelling, for example, through what were once similarly Stygian surroundings between Wolverhampton and West Bromwich on the Great Western Railway might succumb to the sun-kissed temptations of Torquay or Weston-super-Mare.

These pictures were removed, framed and placed on the walls of homes right across the country. It is ironic to think that originals in good condition are now worth a King's ransom. One enterprising fellow found that furniture makers would pay good prices for horsehair. The railways stuffed their seats with this material and so he raided Great Central Railway carriage sidings just outside Marylebone station in London, walking off with sacks of horsehair – until the police caught him.

The railways need all manner of materials for their infrastructure and their operations, and many of these were, or still are, well worth the trouble of stealing. It is by no means unknown for stations and other buildings to have the lead stripped from their roofs. Canvas sheets and tarpaulins used to be required in vast numbers for covering freight wagons. They were also wanted illicitly for a wide range of other, non-railway, purposes, hence there was always a ready sale for these items. The farming fraternity in particular found them extremely useful for covering clamps of root crops and haystacks, for example. In 1951 the Eastern Region of British Railways had over 10,000 sheets missing and it was probably no coincidence that it served an area where there were large amounts of arable land.

Steam locomotives had copper fittings which were always worth stealing. When steam locomotives were being withdrawn in huge numbers in the 1960s they were frequently stored in sidings awaiting the call to be scrapped.

The huge steam engine 'graveyard' at Barry Docks in 1970. These hulks rusted away for years, stripped of anything removable by genuine preservationists and also trophy-hunters. Miraculously many of these locomotives were rescued and have been restored to working order on Britain's heritage railways.

Obscure rural locations were often found with a view to avoiding the attention of metal thieves, but usually with little success, and the valuable portable non-ferrous parts might be removed and spirited away quickly and quietly. Lots of so-called railway enthusiasts entered engine sheds and brazenly stole number plates and nameplates, the latter in particular sometimes fetching five-figure sums in the twenty-first century.

A real bonanza for the criminal community was the development of electric traction and electric signalling, because these both used substantial amounts of copper. Conduits containing copper wire for signalling purposes run by the track through both town and country. Especially in the more rural areas these were, and remain, a tempting target for well-equipped thieves, causing signalling failures and considerable aggravation, not least because of the delays caused to trains. In 2007 the theft of valuable metal from railway property caused more than 2,500 hours of delay to train services, never mind the cost of replacing the materials involved.

No.6400, a 64xx 0-6-0PT of the sort that was hijacked from Wolverhampton Stafford Road engine shed. These diminutive locomotives were introduced in 1932 by the Great Western Railway and designed for working light passenger trains, particularly on branch lines. The Great Western Railway had huge numbers of locomotives of basically the same design and they were often referred to by enthusiasts as 'matchboxes'; sometimes with affection but otherwise with low-key contempt, probably because they were so commonplace.

There have been attempts over the years to joyride on locomotives. One such incident occurred in January 1961 when a small 0-6-0 Pannier Tank numbered 6422 was stolen from Stafford Road shed at Wolverhampton by a former fireman who, at the time, was wanted by the police for questioning in connection with a robbery. At dead of night he found the locomotive unattended, told the man controlling the exit road that the engine was on its way to Worcester Works for maintenance purposes and set off along the main line.

He chugged merrily along through the night, being passed from one signalling section to the next without any suspicion being raised, and he even halted at Stourbridge Junction to take on water. At Droitwich, No.6422 was switched into the loop in order to allow a fast fitted freight train to overtake it. For whatever reason the locomotive was abandoned there and the fireman ran away into the dark. One version of the story goes that back at the shed, no one realised that No.6422 was missing until a footplate crew turned up early in the morning to prepare it for a passenger turn. They searched the shed high and low and then reported to an incredulous foreman that they could not find it.

Another version is that the fireman had followed the correct procedure at Droitwich and had gone to the signal box to sign the train register. Soon afterwards the firemen disappeared into the night, and with the fast freight having gone past the signalman gave No.6422 the road. When the engine did not move the signalman investigated and found that, incredibly, it had had no crew! He then reported his discovery to control. The fireman was charged with obstruction and theft – not of the locomotive but of the coal that was used to get it to Droitwich.

At Chester General one October day, also in 1961, train spotters were admiring a Stanier 'Coronation' 4-6-2 No.46243 *City of Lancaster* at the south end of the station when a Churchward 'Mogul' No.7341 appeared light engine from the direction of Chester Midland shed. Train spotters were used to such movements, but one of them spotted that this was different – there was no one on the footplate! Fortunately the locomotive was travelling slowly and station staff were quickly alerted and able to bring No.7341 to a halt. The authors have been unable to ascertain whether the cause of the runaway was negligence on the part of the footplate crew or someone wilfully either starting to take it for a joyride and then, getting cold feet, abandoning the engine to its own devices. It seems extraordinary that there were no conflicting points and that it managed to get as far as it did.

A disgruntled anonymous railwayman based at Crewe North engine sheds used to send letters to the management of the London & North Western Railway saying that he was going to 'liberate' one of their locomotives by releasing it to chug off along the line by itself. As was intended, this caused chaos on the line and, fortunately only on one occasion, it led to serious injury to a railwayman. The miscreant managed this operation no fewer than nineteen times before attempting it once too often being arrested, charged, found guilty and sentenced to a term in prison. He was an engine driver who obviously had the requisite skills but he never revealed the reasons for his irresponsible behaviour.

Over the years railway offices have consistently received the attention of burglars determined to rifle safes for the day's takings, or extract parcels and packages with valuable contents. These could be highly lucrative. A break-in at Berkhamsted in Hertfordshire in 1956 meant that the robbers left £500 better-off. At least one such burglary nearly ended tragically. In February 1956 a police officer apprehended and arrested two men engaged in robbery at a goods depot at West Hartlepool. They stabbed him, inflicting life-threatening injuries, but fortunately he survived. The two men involved therefore faced far less serious charges than if the injuries had been fatal.

A number of stations and other railway buildings, particularly those in rural locations, have attracted the attention of a different kind of thief – the stripper of lead – especially from roofs. Such criminals were no mere opportunists but needed to be well organised, having transport and all the equipment necessary to carry away their extremely heavy but valuable booty. Coins of the realm are usually heavy and bulky relative to their value but this has not deterred a number of light-fingered characters whose criminal speciality was

A recent view of Berkhamsted station, Hertfordshire. It is good to see handsome old buildings like these adapted for modern use. A lick of paint would not go amiss though.

breaking into the coin machines that controlled entry to the cubicles in station toilets.

The vulnerability of stations to breaking and entering is shown by the fact that in 1961 British Transport Police recorded no fewer than 352 cases of such criminal enterprise. The fact is that just about anything not nailed down was, or still is, grist to the mill of petty and professional thieves on or around railway premises. Actually, nailing it down has never been a guarantee it would not be stolen. If it is valuable, it is also vulnerable.

One extraordinary robber enjoyed a criminal career of several months in the 1930s. He was a young man employed on the London & North Eastern Railway as an engine cleaner. For reasons best known to himself he hit on the idea of taking a railway journey in an otherwise empty compartment, and when the train was in motion he would open the door and embark on a daredevil walk along the footboards, deriving great amusement from the looks of startled amazement on the faces of the passengers as he leered at them through the carriage windows. In fact it was so much fun that he did it

'Take the front cab in the rank, please.'

several times but then decided that the acrobatic stunt could be put to more profitable ends.

Equipping himself with an imitation firearm and wearing a highwayman's mask, he clambered out on the footboards once more and made his way along the outside of the train until he found a traveller alone in a compartment. Such a passenger would have been understandably terrified as someone resembling Claude Duval opened the carriage door, clambered in and demanded money with menaces. Amazingly, he managed to carry out a number of these robberies, but he did so once too often and was caught.

CHAPTER TWO

MURDER ON THE LINE 1840-1900

The Murder of Thomas Briggs

Where better to start than with the first murder on a moving train in Britain? This provoked what – up to then – was the greatest manhunt in British legal history.

You have to imagine Mr Thomas Briggs. He was an aldermanic figure, the epitome of Victorian middle-class respectability. In 1864 he was sixty-nine years of age, tallish, silver-haired, immaculately dressed and sporting a flowing white beard. Altogether, he was a most distinguished-looking gentleman. He was the chief clerk of Robarts, Lubbock & Co., a banking house in the City of London, a position which he had only obtained through a long career of diligent duty and unassailable probity.

He was wearing the kind of clothes he normally wore when travelling to and from work. These included a distinctive high silk hat. He also had an expensive-looking gold chain stretched across his capacious midriff, the chain being attached to a fine gold watch in his waistcoat pocket. He carried a bag in one hand, and a stout walking stick in the other.

On 9 July 1864, a Saturday, he left the office around half-past four and travelled to Peckham, south of the Thames, for dinner with his niece and her husband. Briggs was a widower and he made the pilgrimage to No.23 Nelson Square, now Furley Road, every week. They ate well. They always did. It was still light at half-past eight when he left, his bag now empty because its contents had consisted of little presents for the niece of whom he was very fond. He boarded a horse-bus back to King William Street in the City. He then walked briskly (that was his way; he was very fit and strong for his age), to

Fenchurch Street station where he climbed into a first-class compartment on a train of the North London Railway.

He caught the train with a couple of minutes to spare but no one else joined him in the compartment at Fenchurch Street. The train pulled out five minutes late at 9.50p.m. to start the roundabout route to his destination at Hackney via Shadwell, Stepney and Bow. Much of the route ran on low viaducts which gave a bird's eye view of the rooftops of poor inner-city housing and the myriad of small, often rather noxious, industrial premises and workshops then so characteristic of that part of London's East End. Hackney, however, was a cut above, boasting a respectable gentility.

The North London Railway had only just over thirteen miles of its own line, but its trains also ran on over fifty miles of line belonging to other companies. The North London Railway had an importance out of all proportion to its size because its small network linked the main lines coming into London from the north and west with the City and with the docks in the east. Its first London terminus was at Fenchurch Street via the circuitous route taken by the train conveying Briggs, but later it opened up services running more directly into the Broad Street terminus. This was a substantial station adjacent to Liverpool Street and which stood where the Broadgate development now is.

It may have been a small company but it was a proud one, and it had little time for the lower end of the travel market. Until 1875 it only catered for first and second-class passengers. It possessed a fleet of small but powerful 4-4-0 tank engines and its four-wheeled carriages were quite luxurious by the standards of the time.

It was a warm evening and almost totally dark as the train trundled along. A weak light in the ceiling provided only partial illumination. Briggs had worked all day, had eaten well, and was dozing fitfully. At Bow he exchanged brief pleasantries through his open carriage window with an acquaintance called Lee, who later averred that there were two other passengers in the compartment. One he described as thin and dark, the other as stoutish, thickset and lightly whiskered. Lee remembered being mildly surprised to see Briggs travelling at such a late hour. He was also surprised by the appearance of the other occupants of the carriage; they did not look like first-class passengers. Later, when he was in the witness box, he admitted that he had had a drink or two in a local pub. The general feeling in court was that 'a drink or two' actually meant several, or even many, drinks.

The train pulled out of Bow, being due to arrive at the next stopping place, Victoria Park, Hackney Wick, in a few minutes. The train was now four minutes behind time. The next compartment to that occupied by Briggs was also first class and was occupied by a draper called Withall and a female traveller. They were not together. As the train was approaching Hackney, Withall described how he heard a sudden and strange howling noise, reminiscent of a dog in distress. His unknown female companion made a remark to the same effect. In another compartment close by, a female passenger had the unpleasant experience of being spattered with drops of blood that came in through the open window. She later said that she had heard no untoward noises.

When the train arrived at Hackney, two young men-about-town, Henry Verney and Sydney Jones, were waiting to join the train to travel to Highbury, and they stepped into the compartment in which Briggs had started his journey. It was empty but, although it was very poorly lit, they soon realised that a lot of blood was scattered around the compartment. A number of personal items could be seen. These were a black leather bag and a walking stick. Under the seat lay a black beaver hat, so squashed that it looked as if someone had stood on it. Thoroughly alarmed, they managed to get the attention of the guard who directed them to another compartment.

The guard was intensely irritated by this turn of events. The train was already late and the North London Railway prided itself on the punctuality of its trains. He gave the compartment a quick visual going-over, enough to make it obvious to him that it had very recently witnessed foul play. He locked the compartment and gave instructions for a telegraph message to be sent to the superintendent at Chalk Farm, the station where the train terminated. There the carriage was uncoupled and shunted into a siding to await examination by the police.

Meanwhile the driver of a train proceeding in the opposite direction saw a dark object lying close to the track near the bridge over the 'Duckett Cut'. This waterway, more correctly known as Sir George Duckett's Canal, joined the Lea Navigation to the Regents Canal at Old Ford. It had opened in 1830. The train was brought to a halt and the guard, engine driver and firemen all descended to track level to investigate. They found that the object was the body of a man, battered, bloodied and still alive, although only just.

With considerable difficulty, they carried him down to the street where they were fortunate to encounter a police officer going around his beat. He summoned assistance and a doctor was soon on the scene. His initial impression was that the injuries on the left-hand side of the man's head had probably been sustained by his fall from a train. However, two violent blows had fractured his skull. Briggs's inert body was first of all taken to a nearby pub which did unusually good trade as the news got around. It was later transported to his home in Clapton Square where he died late the next evening. He never regained consciousness.

This horrible murder stirred up a hornets' nest of outraged headlines and articles in the newspapers. 'Murder on the Iron Way' thundered one newspaper truthfully, while another, tending more to hyperbole asked, 'Who is safe? If we

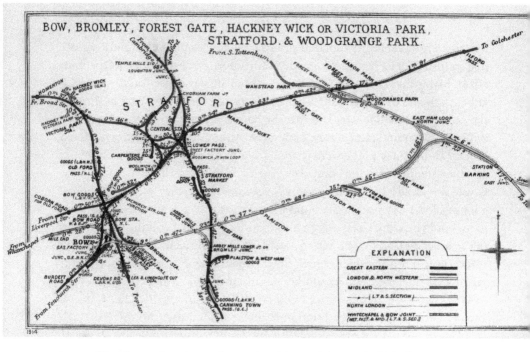

A map of the nineteenth-century railway network in London's East End. The line carrying Muller and Briggs enters from Fenchurch Street on the bottom left and then proceeds through Old Ford and Homerton. Note the complexity of the lines in the Bow and Stratford areas.

may be murdered thus we may be slain in our pew at church, or assassinated at our dinner table'. This first railway murder emphasised just how vulnerable passengers in compartments could be to the depredations of malefactors, even in the biggest city in the world.

They dared not leap from the train while it was in motion. They had no means of stopping the train. It was not easy to attract the attention of the guard or the men on the footplate. Without a side corridor in the carriage, it was hard to attract the attention of travellers in other compartments. Equally there was little that such travellers could do even if they had been alerted to possible trouble. Now two passengers travelling in the same compartment, but who were strangers, would spend the journey eying each other up suspiciously, making sure valuable possessions were out of sight. The manufacturers of coshes, then generally known as life-preservers, now had their workers slaving away feverishly on overtime in order to keep up with demand.

Inspector Tanner and Sergeant Clarke were appointed to the case and were soon certain that the motive for the attack had been robbery. On being examined, the compartment in which Briggs had travelled showed all the signs of having witnessed a murderous assault. Splashes and even pools of blood were on the floor and on the seats. A small travelling bag and a stout walking stick were to be seen under the seat. There was some bloody smearing on the silver knob of the stick. The crushed beaver hat lying on the floor was examined. It had a maker's name. The address was 49 Crawford Street in Marylebone.

It was quickly established that Brigg's valuable gold watch and chain were missing as well as his high silk hat, a 'topper', itself valuable – there was always a ready black market for such expensive fashion items. However, a diamond ring, a silver snuffbox, four sovereigns and some small change had not been taken, suggesting that Briggs's assailants, if there were two of them, had not had time to complete the robbery. It seemed likely that the crushed beaver hat belonged to one of the assailants. They thought that the missing hat belonging to Briggs would prove easy to trace. He had had it specially made by a well-known hatter in Cornhill, in the City. The beaver hat was also distinctive, having a low, flat crown and was rather downmarket compared with Briggs's headwear. Descriptions of the missing items were circulated along with appeals for information.

At first the only lead seemed to be provided by a Robert Death who, perhaps understandably, pronounced his name as 'Deeth'. He worked in a jeweller's and pawnbroker's shop in Cheapside, not far from where Briggs was employed in Lombard Street. The shop was run by his brother and the name 'Death' was used in advertising and packaging.

He told Tanner and Clarke that on the morning of 11 July, that is, the first working day after the attack on Briggs and his subsequent death, a young, somewhat sallow man with a foreign accent came into the shop and exchanged a rather fine gold watch chain for another watch chain and a ring which came to the same value. Something had struck him as fishy about the young man and the transaction they had carried out. Reading about the robbery and subsequent murder in the newspapers, he decided to talk to the police.

It was not much of a start. For a whole week little further information came in and the trail, if indeed it had ever existed, seemed to have gone cold. A week later, on 18 July, it suddenly got much hotter owing to the sharp-wittedness of a London cabbie by the name of Matthews. He was waiting for business in the rank outside the Great Western Hotel which fronted Paddington station. The cabbies had been buzzing – as indeed had all of London – with rumours and speculation about the sensational murder just over a week previously.

They were discussing a poster, of which there were thousands plastered over London, giving such details as were known about the murder and offering a reward of £300 for information that would lead to the arrest of the miscreant or miscreants involved. Matthews read the poster, seemingly for the umpteenth time, when suddenly something clicked. The poster mentioned Robert Death, the jeweller's assistant and the foreign-sounding client. The same name 'Death' had been inside a small box presented to his daughter a few days earlier by a young German man she knew. His name was Franz Muller and he frequently wore a beaver hat. He had at one time been engaged to another of Matthews's daughters.

All this came to Matthews in a rush, and, mixing good citizenship with licking his lips at the prospect of a reward, he set off immediately for his home in the Lisson Grove area to see if he could find the box that Muller had given to his daughter. He found it and took it to the local police station. He gave the police a description of Muller, and even a photograph, which got them quite excited. They became less excited when he told them not to bother searching London for Muller because he had just left England for New York and a new life in the United States of America. This was something he had apparently been talking about for a while. When Death was shown the photograph of Muller, he felt almost certain that it was the foreign-sounding young man he had done business with.

However, the police now had something to work on, and they quickly found out that Muller had pawned a number of objects, including the watch chain he had obtained from Death's shop in order to raise the fare as a steerage passenger on the sailing ship *Victoria* bound for New York from the London Docks. They also discovered that he had written a letter just after the *Victoria* had put to sea which had been delivered to a married couple living in Old Ford with whom he had lodged for several weeks. They went to see the couple whose surname was Blyth.

They revealed that on the night of the murder, Muller had, unusually for him, not returned by eleven o'clock. They had waited up but decided to go to bed, and Muller had clearly let himself in and must have gone to bed in his usual quiet manner. When he came down to breakfast he was his normal cheerful, even charming, self. He was a model lodger described as well-behaved and inoffensive, and the Blyths had been sorry to see him go. On the day after the attack on Briggs Muller had stayed in all day and had gone out with the Blyths that evening. The next day, Monday, he had shown the Blyths a gold chain which he said he had bought cheaply from a man who worked on the docks.

The police were soon gathering a lot of useful information. Matthews and his wife were able to confirm that the crushed beaver hat did indeed belong to Muller. From a German couple called Repsch, living in Aldgate, they learned that Muller had arrived from Cologne about two years previously and they had helped him to get a job working for a tailor in Threadneedle Street. He had been a good worker but he had left on 2 July, stating his intention of emigrating to the USA where he thought he could make a fresh start.

The last time Repsch had seen Muller he had been in high spirits, showing off a watch and chain and a ring which he said he had bought for a good price from a man on the docks. He was also wearing a very fine hat which they had not seen him wearing before. He told them that his other one had been damaged and that he had obtained a replacement of a very superior sort at a bargain price.

Another witness to whom the police spoke was John Hoffa, a friend and workmate of Muller. When Muller had left his digs with Mr and Mrs Repsch he had lodged for a few nights with Hoffa in his room before making for the London Docks to board *Victoria*. With these and various other snippets of information, Tanner and Clarke now felt that there was a case against Muller. At the very least they needed to get hold of him so that he could 'help them with their enquiries', a wonderful euphemism.

Late on the Tuesday afternoon they went to the Chief Commissioner of Police who recognised the need to act quickly, especially in the light of public outrage about the atrocity and the necessity of bringing its perpetrator to justice. He authorised the two officers to sail to New York from Liverpool on the *City of Manchester*, a steam vessel and a much faster ship, in order to be there to arrest Muller when *Victoria* docked. The seriousness with which this case was being taken was indicated by the fact that Robert Death and Matthews accompanied Tanner and Clarke in order to confirm Muller's identity when he was apprehended. The police even gave Mrs Matthews, who had four young children, financial compensation for the loss of her husband's earnings while he was being a good citizen enjoying an expenses-paid passage to New York and back.

New York was buzzing with excitement about the murder, and its citizens were very taken up by the idea that Muller was crossing the Atlantic in order to evade justice, and that following hotfoot and actually overtaking the oblivious Muller was the epitome of cutting-edge technology, a steamship, carrying doughty British detectives determined to bring their quarry to justice. In fact so excited were some New Yorkers that a boatload of them sailed past *Victoria* as she was entering harbour shouting out phrases like, 'How are you, Muller the murderer?' Fortunately for the authorities, Muller apparently did not hear the commotion they made.

Muller must have been musing about the opportunities that the New World would provide for an enterprising young fellow like himself as his ship neared its destination. *Victoria* docked on 26 August. Blissfully unaware of the nemesis bearing down on him as he waited to disembark, no one could have been more surprised than he when a couple of New York uniformed policemen, and a pair of what were clearly English plain-clothes detectives, shouldered their way through the crowd and arrested him.

He was taken below and he and his belongings were searched. On his person were Briggs's gold watch and silk hat which had been slightly altered by Muller. The police officers learned that Muller had made something of a name for himself on the voyage by his truculent and overbearing manner, and had come off second best in a fight with a fellow passenger who he called various rude names. Muller for his part received a corker of a black eye. Fights among the bored passengers on the long voyage were by no means uncommon, but

Muller had also drawn attention to himself by betting that he could eat five pounds of German sausages at one sitting. He laid the bet in order to raise some money but failed in this culinary marathon and, having no cash, paid his debt with two shirts. It seems there had not been a dull moment while Muller was on board!

After the positive identification that was required, extradition proceedings were started, but they quickly ran up against an unexpected snag. There were many rich and influential people of German origin in and around New York and they took up Muller's case, arguing that he was beyond the jurisdiction of the British courts and British police. One argument was that in the USA a person was presumed innocent until proven guilty, whereas Muller had been chased halfway across the world, intimidated by the police and the legal authorities, and was now being threatened with extradition as if the case against him was already decided.

It should be remembered that the general mood of people in the north of the USA was hostile to Britain, because many wealthy Britons supported the Confederate cause in the American Civil War. In fact Britain and the USA were almost in a state of undeclared war.

However, extradition formalities were eventually concluded on 3 September, and Tanner and Clarke embarked on *Etna* with Muller in handcuffs and with Matthews and Death, who had been revelling in the experience of a lifetime, something to tell their grandchildren about – all at public expense. Even Muller clearly enjoyed his voyage back to Blighty. Travelling in *Etna* was a much more luxurious experience than steerage in *Victoria*, and Muller did not stint on the best cuisine that the ship's galley could provide. Neither did he waste his time in between meals. He got to grips with, and completed, a reading of *Pickwick Papers* and *David Copperfield*.

The ship docked at Liverpool on 16 September and, after staying in the city overnight, the party travelled down to London via Crewe and Rugby on the main line of the London & North Western Railway. It was Muller's last journey by train. He was unprepared for the reception he received when he got to London, where ravening crowds jeered and booed him as he was taken first to Bow Street Magistrates' Court where he was committed for trial and then to Holloway Prison.

The trial at the Central Criminal Court, better known as the Old Bailey, began on 27 October 1864. Muller looked small, even frail, and was neatly turned out. He spoke confidently when required and was punctilious with regard to the court's etiquette. He certainly did not look like a man capable of launching a murderous attack on Briggs who may have been considerably older, but was also larger, strongly built and very fit for his age. If Muller had had an accomplice, who was he? Was it Muller and the second, unknown man who Lee had seen at Bow, sharing the carriage with the defendant? He

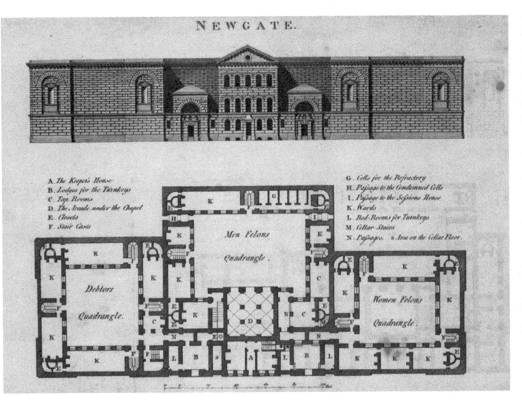

The frontage of Newgate Prison. Over the years up to 1868, this hated building housed tens of thousands of felons, eking out their miserable last days before going off to be executed at Tyburn, near the present-day Marble Arch. After 1783 they were executed instead outside Newgate in the street known as Old Bailey.

stubbornly stuck to the assertion of his total innocence and refused to implicate anyone else.

The witnesses for the prosecution were a motley and unimpressive lot whose reliability and integrity were effectively called into question by the counsel for the defence. The evidence was largely circumstantial but the jury found him guilty, taking just fifteen minutes in their deliberations. The German community in Britain now moved into action, protesting that there had been a miscarriage of justice, producing petitions and pleading for clemency.

However, the time of the execution was set for eight in the morning of 14 November. The location was outside the hated Newgate Prison. The executioner was William Calcraft. He had started his grisly work in 1829 and, despite a long career in the terminatory business, as it were, he was never much of a craftsman and he was unpopular not only with his victims, which was understandable, but also with hanging aficionados. This was because his estimation of how much drop to use for each hanging was poor, and many of

Preparations being made for an execution outside Newgate Prison. Such events often took on the character of a popular carnival, especially if the condemned prisoner was especially hated for the nature of his crimes, or equally for perverse reasons, admired by the gallows crowd.

those whose lives he terminated took longer than necessary to die. Even those who attended every possible hanging believed that the executioner had the responsibility to minimise the condemned prisoner's sufferings.

The crowds that gathered at hangings were known for being boisterous and badly behaved, but the impending death of Muller seems to have attracted the most bestial and wretched of London's population, totalling something like 50,000, baying for blood and avid for entertainment. As *The Times* reported, the crowd went quiet only as Calcraft did his work and Muller's life ebbed away, when there was an awed hush. For the rest of the time there was 'loud laughing, oaths, fighting, obscene conduct and still more filthy language'.

In fact so horrible was the behaviour of the crowd at the execution of Muller that the event undoubtedly contributed greatly to the developing feeling that executions should be made private affairs behind prison walls. Indeed it was only three years later that the last public hanging in England took place, again outside Newgate Prison.

It has entered the annals of folklore that Muller was goaded into making a last-minute admission of guilt by the pastor attending him. Whether or not

Franz Muller.

The handcuffs used on Franz Muller when he was arrested. (Courtesy of Philip Hutchinson)

this is true, it is unlikely that any modern court would have passed such a verdict with the forensic and other investigative techniques now available.

Who got the £300 reward money? It was Jonathan Matthews. It has to be said that his action gave the police enquiries the kick-start they needed, and that without him those enquiries might not have really got started at all. He was, however, one of those people who somehow exuded an air of shiftiness and mendacity. The police took an instant dislike to him and he cut

SHOWING WHAT A WONDERFUL IMPROVEMENT THE HOLES IN THE RAILWAY CARRIAGES ARE, PARTICULARLY DURING THE HOLIDAYS.

Cartoonist's view of a 'Muller Window'.

a particularly poor figure in the witness box under relentless pressure from the defence counsel. Just after the Muller case Matthews was imprisoned for debt and much of the £300 went to pay off his creditors.

Muller had modified the hat he had stolen from Briggs into a kind of cut-down topper and these became fashionable among young men-about-town in London; 'Muller' hats enjoyed several years as fashion items.

On a positive note, some good can be said to have come of the murder of Thomas Briggs in that methods of communication between passengers and what would now be called 'train crew' began slowly to come into use across the railway system. These went under the generic name of 'communication cord' and when activated they notified the engine driver to stop the train as soon as it was safe to do so, but it was many years before such systems became mandatory.

At least one observer commented that a communication cord would not have saved the life of Briggs. The first blow to his head had probably rendered him unable to summon assistance. The London & South Western Railway put small openings, rather like portholes and known as 'Muller windows' in the dividing wall between compartments, and these at least offered some opportunity for frightened passengers to attract attention. Unfortunately these were often used by 'peeping toms' to observe the antics of courting couples.

In the words of the counsel for the prosecution, 'The crime…is almost unparalleled in this country. It is a crime which strikes at the lives of millions. It is a crime which affects the life of every man who travels upon the great iron ways of this country… a crime of a character to arouse in the human breast an almost instinctive spirit of vengeance.' The first British railway murder may have been a long time coming, but when it did it chilled and horrified the entire nation and, as we have seen, it had repercussions which crossed the Atlantic.

A Feckless Murderer

What does a murderer look like? Even a casual acquaintance with the history of crime makes it quite clear that there is no stereotype of the murderer in appearance or possibly in much else.

That aside, Percy Mapleton, who we shall refer to by his alias of 'Lefroy', definitely did not look like a killer. He was a generally rather nondescript man of feeble physique who possessed an aversion to hard work. He was a writer in a small way, with a few minor publications and plays to his name. His problem was one that he shared with many others. He had no regular income, and even when he got a small royalty he no sooner received the money than he spent it. Consequently he was more or less permanently broke. For most of the time he somehow just managed to keep his head above water, but 1881 was not his year and by June he was at his wits' end. He pawned a few personal items and raised a few shillings. Desperate measures were needed if he was not to starve.

Knowing that he was neither strong nor of ferocious appearance, he had managed to get hold of a real working revolver which he intended to use for the purpose of robbery. If he threatened people with the gun, they would quickly surrender their valuables and there would be no need for messy violence in which he might come off second best, or so he reasoned. Where should he look for victims? He could not simply walk down the street brandishing the revolver, and he did not fancy lurking in some dark alley loitering with intent. He hit on the idea of a compartment on a moving passenger train.

On 27 June he headed for London Bridge station and bought a ticket for a train going to Brighton on the London, Brighton & South Coast Railway. He paced up and down the platform looking for a compartment with only one occupant. Preferably his intended victim would look as if he or she was worth robbing and would be likely to co-operate quickly when being threatened with a pistol. Lefroy found his victim.

An elderly gentleman sat alone in a compartment, intent on reading his newspaper and totally oblivious to the impending horrible fate that awaited him. His name was Frederick Gold. He lived in Brighton, and, although largely retired from business, he maintained an interest in a shop in London so he travelled up to town every Monday. He would go to the shop, examine the books, talk to the manager and receive a share of the takings in the form of banknotes. He either banked these straight away or put them in his wallet. He enjoyed Mondays. They kept him in touch with the world of work and he usually made a few social calls at the same time.

On this particular Monday, Gold arrived at London Bridge before ten in the morning. He was, as always, smartly turned out. In a pocket was a trusty watch which went everywhere with him. Engraved on the back was the name 'Griffiths' and the number 16261. On this occasion his share of the takings was £38 5s 6d, of which he banked all but the shillings and pence. He got back to London Bridge around two in the afternoon, found himself an empty compartment and sat back contentedly, drawing on a rather fine cigar and perusing the daily newspaper. He had exchanged a few pleasantries with the ticket collector as he headed for the platform and had nodded to another member of the station staff as he had settled down in his compartment.

Gold would have been less than pleased when another passenger joined him and sat down opposite. He did not acknowledge the newcomer but if he had he might well have noticed that he looked tense and excited. The train pulled out on time and rumbled over the viaducts of Bermondsey which gave a bird's-eye view of the factories, warehouses and other industrial premises which were then such a feature of this part of south-east London. Soon there was plenty of greenery to be seen as the train traversed the leafy developing suburbs such as Forest Hill and Sydenham. South of Croydon it entered Merstham Tunnel.

It was in the blackness of this tunnel that Lefroy decided to launch an attack on his unsuspecting fellow passenger. A passenger in another compartment nearby heard four explosions as the train was passing through the tunnel. He wondered why they should be using fog signals or detonators on a clear day and inside a tunnel but he gave the matter little more thought, and, as the train emerged into the daylight, returned to the penny dreadful he was reading.

A line-side observer near Horley noticed two men apparently engaged in a struggle as the train passed but thought it pointless to report the matter at the local station. Eventually the train reached Preston Park in the northern suburbs of Brighton where Lefroy got off. He was a terrible sight. He was bleeding and had bloodstains on his clothes which were ripped and tattered. Even his collar was missing as he staggered, clearly in pain, down the platform. Passengers were nudging each other and indicating in his direction. He seemed to be in a daze when a ticket inspector stopped him and pointed out that he had a pocket watch dangling from his shoe. Rather feebly Lefroy explained that he had put it there for safe keeping.

The excuse that he gave for his extraordinary appearance and the presence of a watch in an unwonted place was that just before the train left London Bridge two men had entered his compartment. He had not liked the look of them. One was elderly while the other looked like a countryman probably aged about fifty. One or both of them, he said, had set about him in Merstham Tunnel, and although he had fought back he had been knocked insensible and had only recovered consciousness as the train pulled into Preston Park.

On the matter of where these two assailants had gone, he was unable to comment. The bemused man allowed himself to be taken first to answer questions from the police and make a statement and then, with a police escort, to a nearby hospital to have his injuries seen to. He returned in the London direction, telling the police there that he was going to stay with a relation of his at Wallington near Croydon. Two burly constables went with him just to make sure.

By this time, what turned out to be Gold's hat had been discovered by the side of the track and at Hassocks his umbrella had been found. At a quarter to four Gold's body was found near Balcombe Tunnel. It had sustained frightful injuries. One bullet wound and various knife wounds could be seen, and it was evident even to an amateur that this gory corpse was that of a man who had been engaged in a life-and-death struggle. Somewhat later a detached collar was found which was later matched with Lefroy's shirt.

A manhunt was now on, and the police quickly visited the house in Wallington. There they were told that Lefroy had gone to see a local doctor. In fact he must have known that the police would come looking for him and he had gone on the run. He turned up in Poplar in the East End of London, but the police were hot on his trail and he was soon arrested. The case against him was clear and he was found guilty.

As murders go, this had been an uninventive and mundane one. Lefroy was of previously good character and had never shown the least tendency towards

Preston Park station. A recent view.

violence. Clearly he had been driven to desperate measures by his financial plight but it seems quite absurd that he could have thought that he would get away with it. When he left the train at Preston Park he could scarcely have been more conspicuous had he been stark naked. This was not a classic crime nor was its solution a masterwork in the annals of police detective work. The crime was a bit like Lefroy himself – fairly nondescript.

Trouble in the Ranks

Railway employees, or at least those in the front line who have duties that involve them meeting the public, have always been vulnerable to insults, assault and even to murder. Fortunately, it has proved rare for them to assault or even murder each other. However, the Dover Priory station of the London, Chatham & Dover Railway Company was the scenario for just such an incident on 1 May 1868.

Thomas Wells was eighteen years of age and he worked as a carriage cleaner. His supervisor or line manager, as he would now be called, was Edward Walsh. It would not be unfair to say that there was little love lost between them, and mutual antipathy rose to a head when Walsh had instructed Wells a few days

A modern view of Dover Priory station. It takes its name from a nearby medieval monastery. A public school is built on the site and utilises some of the monastic remains.

earlier to deliver a load of manure to his garden. Junior employees were used to taking a fair amount of shit because it went with the territory. Nonetheless, being told to break off his designated duties in order to help Walsh out with his horticultural activities was rightly seen by Wells as evidence that his supervisor was pushing the other aspect of excretory functions to its extreme, and taking the piss.

Seething with rage, Wells went straight from work and bought a pistol and some ammunition. It seems that the next day, or shortly after, he threatened Walsh with the pistol. The latter's response was to tell Wells that his conduct would be reported to the station master. The next morning Wells had the pistol about his person when he went to work and was told to report to the stationmaster. The latter official tried to be conciliatory and suggested that if Wells apologised to Walsh, it would be possible to avoid starting disciplinary proceedings. He then told Wells to leave while he wrote a report on the matter. The report was then read to Wells who was clearly incensed. He knew his job was on the line but it seems that he was past caring.

He stormed over to where he knew Walsh would be and shot him in front of witnesses. Walsh died shortly afterwards. Firing the pistol seems to have assuaged the burning sense of outrage that had motivated Wells to such drastic measures and he seemed confused and cowed by the enormity of his action.

He was found a short distance away, sitting in a railway carriage. The pistol was beside him and he made no attempt to resist arrest.

Little could be offered in mitigation and after a brief trial Wells was condemned to be executed. The sentence was carried out and was perhaps of more significance than the squalid crime itself, because Wells was spared the added humiliation of a public hanging. He was the first felon condemned for a capital offence who was hanged privately behind the walls of a prison.

Murder and Mayhem with Burglary Thrown In

It is said that all human beings have potential for good and for evil. It is not often that we come across a group of men who were not only murderers but brutally, gratuitously violent desperadoes with absolutely no saving graces. However, in 1885 the activities of a gang of four such men were responsible for an outbreak of mayhem around the eastern end of the Solway Firth and down what became known as the West Coast Main Line, all the way from Carlisle to Lancaster. The four men were well known to the police; indeed their case notes would have filled a fair-sized pantechnicon. Their names were Anthony Rudge, John Martin, James Baker and William Baker. The last two, although sharing the same name, were not related. The police regarded them all as exceptionally dangerous.

Events in October 1885 were to show just how ruthlessly vicious and dangerous they could be. Rudge made a speciality of stealing what would now be called 'designer dogs' to order. A hardened recidivist, he mixed stealing dogs with robbery and was then being sought by the police in connection with a robbery at Brixton in south London. Martin was perhaps the most dangerous of the men. He was wanted in connection with the murder of a police inspector who he had shot while evading arrest after a burglary at Romford in Essex. James Baker's speciality was receiving stolen goods and William Baker often used violence when engaged in robbery. All of them were well acquainted with the residential and other facilities of Her Majesty's prisons.

They were career criminals whose activities were usually carried out in urban environments where they could enjoy relative anonymity. Had any police officer been watching them as they congregated at the small Dumfriesshire town of Gretna he could only have come to one conclusion, which was that they were clearly up to no good. Gretna is just north of the river Sark which marked the border between England and Scotland at this point, and it achieved immortality as being the place to which eloping couples from England fled in order to get married, an eighteenth-century Scottish law allowing the ceremony of legal marriage to take place by means of a declaration in front of witnesses.

They had arrived at Gretna on a special train put on for a local sporting event, but it was not sport that they had in mind – it was burglary, and no ordinary burglary at that. They were planning to break into Netherby Hall, the ancestral home of Sir Frederick Graham. They knew that his wife owned some very fine and valuable jewellery, and with their contacts they were certain that they could find a ready market for their booty. Netherby Hall is about two miles north-east of the small market town of Longtown, itself about three miles east of Gretna. The core of the hall is a pele tower, a small fortress which was designed to withstand a short siege, very necessary in the lawless days when these debatable lands were being fought over by the Border Reivers, the ruthless cut-throat gangsters who terrorised the Borders for centuries.

However, the gang had little interest in matters historical when they arrived at Gretna, where their first action was to deposit some cases at the station. They reconnoitred Gretna and its surrounding district as far as Longtown and made some enquiries which elicited the information that the Graham family was in residence at Netherby. The next day James Baker retrieved one of the cases from the left-luggage office at Gretna station.

They spent much of the day in a pub close to the station, and it is probable that the contents of the case had a bearing on the planned burglary because one of the pub's customers saw them apparently engaged in making a wax impression of some keys. The gang were not the kind of people who looked as if they would welcome enquiries about their activities. A sensible man would avoid catching their eyes. The customer discreetly mentioned what he had seen to the pub landlord but the latter was too busy to do anything about it.

It was dark when the gang entered the grounds of Netherby Hall. They broke in without being detected and made their way to the room where Lady Graham kept her jewellery. This was seized and the gang left the scene quickly. The burglary was discovered shortly afterwards. Various precious items were missing and it was clear that a ladder had been used to gain entry. An outraged Sir Frederick was informed. His immediate response was to send a rider to enlist the help of the police while he gathered a posse of grooms, footmen, gamekeepers and other male servants. They proceeded to scour the estate and the whole neighbourhood for the scoundrels who had had the temerity to relieve his wife of her expensive bangles and baubles.

Within an hour all the roads were under observation and two police officers ran into the gang. Without hesitation the gang fired a number of shots into the darkness. The officers were both hit and injured. The gang disappeared. Another officer shortly afterwards stopped them but had to back off when it was clear that they had guns and were prepared to use them. It was about two in the morning when a signalman in an isolated signal box heard footsteps crunching the ballast close by and he was just able to make out three men trudging along the track in the direction of Carlisle. Bravely, but as it turned out unwisely, he left the box and chased them some distance whereupon they turned on him and beat him insensible.

Later on two men were seen in a shunting yard at Carlisle and a blood-stained jemmy was found. There were no more sightings during the day and it looked as if the gang had gone to ground until darkness. It was thought that they were probably still on railway property, perhaps hiding in a wagon somewhere. Carlisle was a major railway centre served by no fewer than six mainline railway companies and there was such an abundance of goods depots and sidings around the city that looking for the men was like looking for a needle in a haystack.

The next sighting was at Southwaite, a small wayside station on the London & North Western Railway Company's main line to the south of Carlisle. There a stranger asked the stationmaster if and when there was a train to London. He seemed displeased with the response and disappeared. The stationmaster had heard about the events of the previous night. He did not like the stranger's appearance and attitude and he telegraphed the railway police.

Shortly afterwards at Plumpton, another small station, the next but one down the line towards Lancaster and London, the stationmaster caught sight of three men acting suspiciously and he also alerted the railway police. Two men, who it turned out were Rudge and James Baker, went into a local pub for refreshment and left rather abruptly, perhaps sensing that their presence was attracting unwanted attention.

Soon after they had left a number of people heard a single shot, and a local man walking his dog heard cries for help from the roadside. It was PC Byrne, the village bobby, whose misfortune it was to have run into Rudge and Baker. They had shot him in the head. His life was ebbing away at the moment of his discovery by the passer-by. There was nothing that could be done for the dying man.

By whatever means, the gang members were managing to make their way southwards because the next sighting was a few miles away at Penrith where a policeman saw three men moving about suspiciously near the railway. It was dark, of course, and they vanished, but he alerted the railway staff who searched a goods train about to depart southwards. The guard was instructed to keep an eye out and no sooner was the train slowly leaving the sidings at Penrith than he saw three men rush out of the line-side shrubbery and climb into one of the wagons.

Not wanting the intruders to think that they had been spotted, the guard acted in a very level-headed way. He wrote messages on pieces of paper, wrapped them round lumps of coal and threw them out as his train passed Shap. This was a common way in which engine drivers or guards tried to contact signalmen or traffic control if they had something they wanted to tell them but did not want to stop the train. It was all a bit hit-and-miss, but by something of a miracle one of these messages was quickly picked up and the Shap signalman telegraphed ahead to Tebay to request that the local police meet the train at that point, ready to arrest the three men.

In fact the constabulary were not there but the railway company had gathered every available man to meet the train. Anyone familiar with the Tebay district will know that life on those northern fells was hard and there were hard men among the reception committee awaiting the arrival of the goods train. These men had equipped themselves with a variety of ersatz but intimidating weapons, mostly tools of their trade, and they proceeded to investigate the train, starting at the engine and working backwards. The noise they made obviously disturbed the gang who took a desperate decision and leapt out of the truck, without warning, hoping to catch their pursuers by surprise.

Martin was chased by the engine driver who proved remarkably fleet of foot but paid for it by being severely injured by Martin when he caught up with him. However, the fugitive quickly found himself surrounded by brawny lads who, by sheer weight of numbers, seized him, pinioned his arms and tied him to a handy telegraph pole before he was able to get his shooter out. Rudge also ran like lightning but was likewise overwhelmed and tied to a telegraph pole. He also did not use his gun.

Why the men did not use their shooters in this dire situation is a mystery. We have already seen that they had been fully prepared to use them and had done so in the last couple of days. James Baker managed to evade his pursuers and must have got into another truck on a different goods train because he was spotted in it by two railway workers at Oxenholme. At Lancaster another railwayman spotted Baker and challenged him. The two of them fought like wildcats and Baker was eventually overcome.

Rudge, Martin and James Baker were taken back to Carlisle under guard. A huge crowd turned out at Citadel station seething with hatred, and only with some difficulty were they prevented from lynching the men. The items of jewellery that the gang had stolen had been jettisoned from the trains they had ridden south on and most were recovered quickly, including the most valuable of them which was known as the 'Diamond Star'. The men were charged with murder and appeared at Carlisle Assizes on 18-20 January 1886. The three of them were found guilty and were hanged at first light on 8 February. William Baker was regarded as an accessory and received a lengthy term of penal servitude.

A memorial was put up in memory of the valour of PC Byrne. It was erected close to Plumpton station. The station closed in May 1948 but the memorial is still in situ. It is a mute reminder of the devotion to duty of a brave man and the profligate and calculating brutality of Messrs Rudge, Martin and the two Bakers.

Murder in the Pursuit of Theft

Most freight traffic conveyed by rail in the twenty-first century moves in container and bi-modal trains. These travel at considerable speed and, even when at a standstill, are hard to break into and enter for the purposes of theft. In the past, however, and even as late as the 1960s and 1970s, many consignments were carried in small wagons and vans. These spent much of their transit time marshalled in trains waiting in loops and sidings for a clear road between trains given greater priority. Equally they might spend hours or days in sidings where they were sorted and marshalled into other trains.

These situations made them very vulnerable to the attentions of thieves. Some consignments such as cigarettes or bottled spirits were highly attractive to the light-fingered fraternity. It is worth remembering that before the growth of the road haulage industry in the 1920s and 1930s, railways had something approaching a monopoly in the conveyance of freight, goods and almost every kind of merchandise across the country.

One of the main concerns of the railway police was to guard consignments against pilfering, whether in warehouses and goods sheds or in wagons moving about or waiting in sidings and yards. Their forces, however, were thinly stretched given the sheer extent of the railway system.

In 1887 there was a spate of breaking into and stealing from wagons waiting in goods sidings at Wigan in Lancashire. A Detective Sergeant in the London & North Western Railway Company's police force, Robert Kidd and a local detective officer called Osbourne were detailed to keep watch. This was nervy if boring work, and the two men were getting fed up; they had had the sidings under surveillance for six weeks without anything untoward happening and nothing to show for their efforts. Perhaps they had been spotted and their presence was deterring the thieves. Perhaps the thieves had simply turned their attentions elsewhere. Regardless the watch had to be maintained and the men met up as usual, this particular occasion being Saturday 29 October.

On this particular night, however, they spotted an intruder. He was a well-known old local lad with the good Lancastrian name of Halliwell. When he was challenged he ran off but Osbourne caught up with him and held him up against a wagon. Another man appeared out of the darkness and he blundered into Kidd and Osbourne who were restraining Halliwell. The newcomer also boasted a good Lancashire name, in this case Kearsley. He too was a regular habitué of the police cells and local courts.

Osbourne had his truncheon at the ready to deal with Kearsley when a third man arrived. Osbourne thought that the new arrival had a weapon and so he aimed a heavy blow with his truncheon at the man's hand. The sidings around goods yards were poorly lit, and in the confused melee that ensued the three men managed to get away, Halliwell running off triumphantly having grabbed Osbourne's truncheon. Where was Kidd?

Osbourne found him nearby on his knees with blood pouring down his face and clearly in a critical state. He tried to help Kidd by moving him but he cried out in pain. Osbourne was exhausted and shaken up but he managed to call for help before himself collapsing. Soon various railway workers and the local police were on the scene. Kidd was found to have appalling injuries. He had been stabbed nine times and had clearly been engaged in a life-and-death struggle.

His assailant or assailants had not only stabbed him but had beaten him repeatedly on his body and his limbs. These injuries proved fatal, Kidd's life ebbing away within the hour. Investigations at the scene produced two blood-stained caps of the sort worn by working men and also evidence that a wagon containing sweets had been broken into. It was unclear whether anything had actually been stolen. A hue-and-cry went out. The search was on for the three men, now wanted for murder.

The Wigan citizenry seems to have been shaken and shocked by the murder of Sergeant Kidd who was well known and well liked, and the police were soon following a number of useful leads provided by the public. These resulted in the quick arrest of the three men. Kearsley and Halliwell have already been mentioned. The third member of this horrible triumvirate was Elijah Winstanley. Dare we say it but he was another with a deeply rooted Lancashire name and, like Halliwell, he was a pitman. The three of them were charged with the murder of Kidd and with assaulting and inflicting grievous bodily harm on Osbourne. Halliwell may have been a pitman, he may have been a recidivist, but he now revealed that he was also a grass. He sang like a canary. It was his attempt to escape the noose.

When the case went to court, it quickly became evident that they were not the individuals or possibly the gang that had been systematically thieving from wagons in the sidings and which Sergeant Kidd had been instructed to investigate. The three men had spent an evening drinking in pubs in the Lower Ince area of Wigan and, probably in their cups, they had then decided to investigate the opportunities for a bit of casual theft offered by the large fan of railway sidings at Springs Branch, close by.

The three ne'er-do-wells appeared before Wigan Magistrates and were then committed to Liverpool Assizes. Halliwell, having turned Queen's evidence, was charged only with unlawful wounding. Curiously the case against him was dismissed on the basis of insufficient evidence. Kearsley and Winstanley appeared on capital charges but the court ruled that the former was only an accomplice to the murderous assault on Sergeant Kidd, and although he was found guilty he was sentenced only to a long term in prison. Winstanley, therefore, was left to face execution. His death was probably no great loss.

However, questions could be asked as to why he was left to give up his life when his associates were every bit as guilty of the murder of Kidd. He left a young wife and seven children.

Unrequited Love

Ernest Keeling was a deeply frustrated young man. When he was a schoolboy, he had, metaphorically at least, carried the school satchel of Amy Lister. As an adult he retained more than fond memories of her, but their paths had parted. She was the headmistress of a school in Devizes, Wiltshire, and he was employed in Birmingham, where they had been brought up and attended school together. He was also a teacher. Such was Keeling's passion for Amy that in 1889 he applied for a job at her school so as to be near her and to attempt to woo her.

It is not known whether or not he got as far as an interview but he certainly got as far as Devizes. He wooed her for all he was worth but without even chipping away at her stony heart. She told him those words that all men dread to hear, 'I like you but only as a friend.' Lover was what Keeling had in mind. He was disappointed and more than a little put out. He hung around her for months hoping for a change of mind, but presumably did not pester her too much because she agreed to travel on a railway excursion with him.

This proved to be an unfortunate decision because she had underestimated the depth of Keeling's passion. They occupied an otherwise empty compartment and he sank to his knees, imploring her to agree to a more physical relationship. We shall never know whether or not she said that she would never have fancied him even if he had been the last man on earth, but whatever she did say stung him so much that he took out a gun and shot his loved one through the head and then pushed her dying body out of the moving carriage. A few seconds later he leapt out of the train and, landing safely, proceeded to blow his own brains out.

Something to get your Teeth into

Wilhelm Arnemann was a German who lived in Nottingham where he had a business making false teeth. He was a man it was difficult to ignore. Something of an eccentric, he insisted on sleeping on the roof of his house even in sub-zero temperatures. It was, however, his readiness to go to law that brought him the reputation of being a stormy petrel. Time and time again he took customers who defaulted on their payments to court, where he always lost the case because the false teeth he made never ever fitted the mouths of the customers concerned. This small technical snag meant that the courts ruled that people who had bought these ill-fitting dentures were perfectly entitled not to pay for such sub-standard items.

A sense of grievance was building up in Arnemann's bosom and it reached a peak when, in November 1889, a judge of the Nottingham Court yet again threw out his claim and presented him with a bill for legal expenses. You can only push a man so far and Arnemann was so piqued that he decided to settle the hash of Judge Bristowe who had made this ruling. He knew that Bristowe regularly caught an early evening train of the Great Northern Railway from the London Road station in Nottingham to his home at West Hallam on the line to Derby Friargate.

On 19 November he shadowed him to London Road and shot the judge in the back at point-blank range as he was climbing into the train. Arnemann was quickly wrestled to the floor and disarmed. It did not mitigate his defence in the subsequent court case that while he was still lying on the platform being held in a vice-like grip he had said, 'I hope I have done for the old man. I should like to drink his blood'. In fact he had not done for Bristowe, who survived, but his assailant received twenty years' penal servitude for attempted murder.

An Unsolved Mystery between Hounslow and Waterloo

The public find murders fascinating. They find unsolved murders even more fascinating. It is likely that 'Ripperology' would never have assumed the proportions of an industry had Jack the Ripper been brought to justice – whoever he was. Certainly those who produce books and television programmes on the subject would not have found it such a lucrative trade. Of course, the fact that these ghastly crimes were perpetrated on prostitutes in the mean streets and labyrinthine alleys of London's East End adds some desirable theatricality and sense of place. Now each year thousands of people who like to be safely scared pound the streets of Whitechapel, visiting the locations where these women had their wretched lives prematurely and bloodily ended. Far less well known was a murder on a suburban train of the London & South Western Railway bound for the company's London terminus at Waterloo.

The year was 1897. Elizabeth Camp was an attractive, intelligent working-class woman aged thirty-three years old. On a cold February day she had been extremely busy. In the morning she had gone to Hammersmith to visit her younger sister and had then travelled on to Hounslow in the early evening for tea with her elder sister, a Mrs Haynes. Elizabeth was shortly to get married and she had been doing some shopping in anticipation of the happy day as well as spending time with her sisters of whom she was very fond. She was therefore feeling happy when she returned to Hounslow station to catch the 7.42 train to Waterloo.

With her sister and a man euphemistically described as a 'friend of the family', she had even managed to fit in a quick drink in a pub not far from Hounslow station. The day was not over because Edward Barry, her fiancé, was going to meet her at Waterloo and they were intending to visit a music hall. She was somewhat encumbered by the parcels and packages containing the items she had bought as she selected and entered an empty second-class compartment. Unfortunately, she was never to leave the compartment alive.

Her fiancé, Edward Berry, was a good-looking and steady young man but a bit of a worrier who tended to fuss and mother-hen Elizabeth. She probably found this mildly irritating since she was a very capable woman herself. She had tried her hand successfully in a number of trades but in 1897 she was the manageress of a busy pub in the Walworth district of south London. As was his way, Edward got to Waterloo in plenty of time to meet Elizabeth's train which was due in at 8.23. He was more than a bit put out therefore when the train arrived but Elizabeth did not hurry through the throng of passengers to greet him. It was most unlike her not to be where and when she said she was going to be.

He was in a bit of a flap. He did not know what to do for the best. What time was the next train from Hounslow due? Had she been on the train but they had somehow managed to miss each other? Was she also wandering around the station, looking for him? We easily forget the difficulties of contacting people in such circumstances before the age of mobile phones and text messaging. Edward fussed here and fussed there, getting more agitated by the minute, before deciding to return to the barrier at the platform where the train that Elizabeth should have been on had arrived. He could not help noticing a knot of agitated-looking railwaymen around the open door of a compartment of the train from Hounslow. The ever-anxious Edward suddenly became even more so. His anxiety intensified as two railway police officers made their way briskly towards the carriage.

It was the custom for cleaners to service the train from Hounslow before it left for another foray into London's burgeoning south-west suburbia. Elizabeth's body was discovered by a cleaner as he opened the compartment door. Her head and torso were largely under the seat with her legs spread widely on the compartment floor. A growing pool of blood was oozing from the corpse. Nowadays the whole of Waterloo station would probably be sealed off and no train movements allowed for at least forty-eight hours.

This was 1897, however, and with scant regard for evidence at the scene the body was lifted out onto the platform. It was a truly gruesome sight. The dead woman had clearly been the victim of an exceptionally brutal attack in which she had been beaten to death and her skull had been staved in. There was blood everywhere, and even to an unpractised eye it was clear that the victim had not gone to her death without a ferocious fight back. The body was removed to the mortuary at St Thomas' Hospital. With his heart in his mouth, fearing the worst, Edward followed. He made it clear who he was and was called upon to identify the battered corpse. The worst-case scenario he could ever have anticipated lay in front of his horrified eyes.

The police scoured the compartment for clues. Apart from it clearly having witnessed a furiously violent physical struggle, the only items that might possibly be of significance were a pair of bone cufflinks on the floor of the compartment near where the body had been lying. It was considered odd that there was no trace of Elizabeth's train ticket but that might have been in the purse which she habitually carried and was nowhere to be found. If the motive was robbery, why had one or two jewellery items of minor value not been taken? Why should a would-be robber pick on a fit-looking youngish woman who was clearly of the working classes? Surely a more affluent but weaker victim could have been found by the unknown assailant had he only exercised some degree of patience.

The salaciously minded quickly homed in on the idea that the motive of the attacker was sex. Cheap, sensational and melodramatic fiction of the Victorian period found a rich seam in the horrible fates that might befall innocent maidens at the hands of male malefactors travelling in the railway compartment carriages of the time. Any male over the age of puberty was a potential sex-fiend stalking railway stations in order to locate vulnerable women travelling alone. Having done so, they of course then subjected them to a fate worse than death.

Those with salacious minds were therefore badly disappointed when it was made clear that Elizabeth had not been sexually assaulted. In fact, attack either for the purposes of robbery or sex seemed strange given that the train from Hounslow stopped at so many stations, hardly providing the time for a successful assault on a woman as fit and strong as Elizabeth had been. However, a murderous attack had clearly taken place. What was the motive of the murderer? Indeed who was the murderer?

The railway police were supported by a team from Scotland Yard headed by Detective Chief Inspector Marshall. He was an old hand and he quickly concluded that since Elizabeth's blood was still warm when her corpse was delivered to St Thomas', she almost certainly had been killed towards the end of the journey from Hounslow and that her attacker had therefore probably left the train at one of the last three stops before Waterloo. These stations were not particularly busy at that time of the evening and Marshall hoped that questioning the staff concerned might provide information about anyone seen with blood-stained clothing or acting in any way suspiciously. The resulting enquiries produced nothing.

The police were at their wits' end and were coming in for something of a roasting from the public because of the lack of any significant developments. This brutal murder had excited widespread indignation and people wanted results. Marshall, in desperation, ordered a minute examination of the track-side on the route taken by the train as it approached London. Between Putney and Wandsworth a heavy porcelain pestle was found. It had blood and human hair adhering to it. The hair had belonged to Elizabeth Camp. The police now had the murder weapon. They issued handbills with a picture of the pestle and appeals to anyone who might recognise it. There was no useful response.

Next they appealed for anyone who had been on the 7.42 train from Hounslow to come forward. The only possible lead was provided by a passenger who volunteered the information that he had seen a man leaving the carriage concerned at Wandsworth. A description was provided and soon afterwards a man who was a dead ringer for it walked into Wandsworth police station and told a startled desk sergeant that he need look no further. With an air of swagger and pride he then announced that he was the murderer. He turned out to be a hoaxer with the mental age of a child. No one else came forward.

Gradually the furore over Elizabeth's murder died down as the popular press found new horrors to feast upon. The police scaled down their enquiries but continued to follow a number of clues. They discovered that Elizabeth had formerly been engaged to a barman called Brown. The relationship had ended very acrimoniously and Brown still resented the way he thought he had been treated. Elizabeth had been receiving a number of anonymous and threatening letters and the police thought that Brown probably wrote them.

One of the issues between the couple had been money. Elizabeth was clearly a very competent financial manager while Brown was a spendthrift. Apparently Brown still owed her money. This would have given him a motive for murder. Having thought that at last they were getting somewhere, the police then had their hopes dashed when Brown turned out to have a cast-iron alibi.

There is a lot of sweat and often little glory in routine police enquiry work. It is their job to uncover information that may be relevant, and in the course of this particular enquiry they found that Elizabeth was something of a moneylender. Such people are, by the very nature of the service they provide, generally disliked. In addition, Berry told them that she frequently carried a substantial amount of money on her person. Could her murderer be someone who had noticed this and had waited for an opportunity to rob her when she was alone?

It turned out that a number of people owed her money. Could it be a robber who was also a creditor? The police turned their attention to Elizabeth's creditors. One of them turned out to be the 'friend of the family' who had joined Elizabeth and her sister for a drink at Hounslow before she had left for what turned out to be her terminal journey. His name was Stone. He explained that he had accompanied Elizabeth and her sister to the pub in Hounslow to celebrate the forthcoming nuptials and then left them to make their way to the station. He said that he had then gone off to do urgent business elsewhere and had not returned to Hounslow until at least four hours later.

Knowing which train Elizabeth was going to travel on, had he doubled back to the station unseen and entered another carriage? Had he then alighted at an intermediate station and, intent on murdering the woman to whom he owed money, joined Elizabeth in her compartment and then committed the dreadful deed between stations? He had the motive and the opportunity. However, the means were something of a problem. It somewhat stretches the bounds of credibility to believe that he was in the habit of carrying a heavy pestle around with him. Or had he secreted it on his person in the foreknowledge that Elizabeth would be visiting Hounslow that day and returning to London on a little-used train?

We will never know. Although Stone looked to have had the motive, the means and the opportunity, the police questioned him for some time and then let him go because they did not have enough evidence to charge him with anything, or so they said. The newspapers of the time were not satisfied and hinted that the public were being kept in the dark for undisclosed reasons. The story really ends there. The murder of Elizabeth Camp on the 7.42 from Hounslow to Waterloo was never solved and obviously never will be.

An Appointment at Newgate

Louisa Masset lived in Bethune Road, Stoke Newington, London N16. She was half-French, half-English and aged thirty-three when she hit the headlines in 1899. Louisa was single and she lived with her married sister and her husband. She had a small boy named Manfred. He was illegitimate and Louisa had left France because of the stigma attached to the mothers of children born out of wedlock there. The child lived with and was looked after by a foster-mother in Tottenham and Louisa saw him regularly. The boy's natural father apparently paid the cost of childcare.

Having the child looked after meant that she worked as a governess, receiving a relatively good wage, and she also taught piano. Louisa had a mind of her own and little respect for conventional mores, truly a liberated 'New Woman' in that sense. A young Frenchman of nineteen called Eudor Lucas moved in next door. Soon the couple were engaged in a steamy sexual relationship, living entirely for the pleasures of the moment and with no romantic notions about loving each other until the day they died.

Quite unexpectedly in October 1899 Manfred's father contacted Louisa requesting that he should take over the job of looking after the boy. This seemed like a good idea for all concerned and she made arrangements to meet Helen, Manfred's foster-mother, and to take him back into her own custody, albeit temporarily. She went out into the garden and took a brick, which she put into a bag, and then she picked the child up on the morning of 27 October and they travelled to London Bridge station. A witness came forward who said that she saw them together in the buffet at about three in the afternoon and the little boy seemed highly distressed. The same witness saw Louisa at around six. She was alone. It transpired that she then went off on a dirty weekend in Brighton with Eudor.

It seems that in between the first and the second time that she was seen at London Bridge she had doubled back to north London. Two ladies entered the waiting room at Dalston Junction on the North London Railway and in the ladies' lavatory they found the naked body of a small boy. Even to their untrained eye it appeared that he had been battered with a brick and then suffocated. The brick was close by in two pieces. The police were called. Statements were made to the press who regaled their readers with every gory detail, real and imagined, and a murder hunt was launched.

On Monday 30 Helen received a letter from Louisa telling her that Manfred was now in France, safe and sound but missing her awfully. All London was buzzing with speculation about the dead boy found at Dalston Junction. Helen was suspicious that the child's description matched that of Manfred and she went to the police. She provided a formal identification of the dead child. A bundle of little boy's clothes had been found at Brighton station and Helen gave these a positive identification as well.

A mass of further evidence was gathered and although Louisa concocted a cock-and-bull story that she had placed Manfred in the care of another foster-mother, the court at the Old Bailey found her guilty and she was hanged at Newgate on the early morning of 9 January 1900 after confessing to the crime. No real reason was adduced about why she murdered her three-year-old son. Perhaps she did it to save on childcare costs. Perhaps she did it because she found her responsibilities for him something of a burden. She clearly did not have a strong maternal streak. Louisa was the first person to be hanged in Britain in the twentieth century.

Caught by the Telegraph

Not a murder on a railway train, nor even a murder on railway premises, but a murder where the perpetrator used the railway in his attempt to escape. Also it was a murder where the telegraph, that new-fangled device used to help safety and communication on the railways, showed how effective it could also be in apprehending a suspect on the run. Let us briefly consider the genesis of the electric telegraph.

Existing methods of communication used particularly in connection with warfare, such as flags and semaphores, were only effective if they could be seen and recognised, and there were many occasions such as darkness and fog, for example, where this was impossible. The earliest hesitant steps in the direction of using electricity for a high-speed form of communication over long distances did not occur in Britain but were on the European continent and also in the USA. By the early 1840s a modification of Samuel Morse's Morse code was widely used on the American railroads when messages had to be sent at high-speed.

In Britain William Fothergill-Cooke created an electrically operated telegraph system and early in 1837 obtained permission to conduct trials in a tunnel on the Liverpool & Manchester Railway. His Heath Robinson-like apparatus was not a great success. Greater results occurred when he teamed up with Charles Wheatstone. On 25 July 1837 messages were successfully sent and received on the section of line of the London & Birmingham Railway from Euston to Camden. Despite this success the London & Birmingham was not convinced of its efficiency over longer distances and was wary of the cost of installing this system along the whole length of its main line.

Our heroes had been elated by the success of the apparatus on Camden Bank and then deflated by its rejection, but nothing loath they set to work to improve it. They did this so effectively that they were able to convince the directors of the Great Western Railway to install the modified system on their main line out of London, initially in 1839 to Hanwell and extended in 1842 to Slough. Now all kinds of messages could be transmitted to assist the safe and efficient running of the Great Western Railway's main line to the west. Other railway companies adopted the Cooke and Wheatstone system and it soon became almost universal across Britain's burgeoning railway system.

Even those who had little interest in railways and no understanding of electricity could not have failed to prick up their ears in 1845 when the telegraph played a vital role in the apprehension of a suspected murderer. John Tawell was a highly intelligent, very personable, persuasive and resourceful man; a devoted worshipper and a social success whose business activities had provided the means for him to have a very comfortable lifestyle. However, as so often happens, behind the respectable veneer there lay a double life.

Those acquaintances who thought they knew him were not aware that when he was scarcely out of his teens he had been sentenced to transportation on conviction for forgery. His behaviour in the Australian penal colony was exemplary and he managed to return to England as a 'ticket-of-leave man', essentially licensed to maintain good behaviour. He quickly insinuated himself into the affections of a rich widow, like him a Quaker, and after they married he had access to her large bank account.

Tawell had a penchant for extra-marital affairs. One of these was with a woman called Sarah Hart who was a former servant of his. After she left his service he set her up in a cottage in Slough, discreetly out of the public eye. He fathered a couple of children with Sarah and accepted financial responsibility for them. He spent the night or occasional weekend at Slough and ensured that she had enough money to buy the things she wanted. The problem was that Sarah, like many kept women, enjoyed spending her keeper's money, this being some compensation for the social ostracism that went with her way of life.

This was all very well until Tawell retired from business and experienced a significant decline in his ready cash. His cash may have declined but Sarah's desire to spend it showed no sign of waning. He thought it unreasonable that she should insist on living in the manner to which she had become accustomed when his own income had fallen. Very quickly their relationship went from tranquil to tempestuous.

If Tawell had ever been in love with Sarah, he had now definitely fallen out of love with her. The relationship had become like an albatross and so he resolved to kill her. He made his preparations with care. On 1 January 1845 he bought some prussic acid at a chemist's shop in the City of London and then cashed a cheque on one of his bank accounts, although he knew he did not have the funds to support it. He called in at a City coffee house where he was known to ascertain what time it closed in the evening. He then headed for Paddington and boarded the four o'clock local train to Slough.

He arrived at Sarah's cottage about five o'clock. It seems that the couple were getting on reasonably well at the time because Sarah made a couple of visits to a local pub to buy some bottles of stout. Later in the evening the mood between Sarah and Tawell changed and neighbours heard them arguing about the children. Tawell wanted Sarah to agree to have them placed with a baby farmer. Shouts and screams of pain followed and Tawell was seen making his way from the cottage clearly in a state of great agitation. Another witness saw him running in the direction of the railway station.

By this time the neighbour had tried to comfort Sarah, who she thought was dying, and had sent for a doctor. Sarah died just about as soon as the doctor arrived to examine her. A local priest was also called and he took his pony and trap to the station as fast as he could go. He realised that Tawell had been on the station and had left on the return train to Paddington. He persuaded the staff to telegraph to Paddington requesting that Tawell be arrested on arrival there. Police officers were waiting for him, but instead of arresting him they followed him to his lodgings.

Obviously by the time Tawell returned to the coffee house in the morning the police had more information about him; they were there waiting for

A Cooke and Wheatstone
electric telegraph apparatus
as used by the Great Western
Railway around 1850.

him and he was arrested. He initially denied having been in Slough on the previous day or even knowing anyone who lived there. In a rather patronising way he told them that his social status put him above suspicion. He was soon disabused on this matter because he was charged with murder.

The trial began on 12 March 1845 at Aylesbury and it excited enormous interest. The evidence suggested that Tawell had somehow managed to place some prussic acid in the stout that Sarah was drinking and it was that poison which had caused her death. On the third day the jury retired to consider their verdict and they took just half an hour to make the decision that Tawell was guilty. Although this was not entirely unexpected the verdict was met with oohs and aahs, and it seems that Tawell, as has been the case with other male murderers, had elicited the adoration of some of the females present in the public area of the court who wept openly and loudly when the sentence of death was pronounced on their hero.

On 28 March Tawell was hanged at Aylesbury. It is unlikely that he would have been found guilty in a modern court on the strength of the evidence

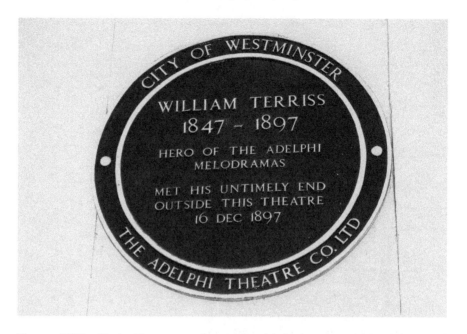

Plaque to William Terriss. He was a popular actor murdered by an insane and unemployed fellow actor outside Covent Garden underground station. His ghost is said to haunt the station itself.

presented. However, the case has retained some fame, less perhaps for the nature of the murder itself than for the fact that Tawell was the first murderer to be apprehended by the authorities using the high-speed communications capability which had just become available courtesy of Cooke and Wheatstone's electric telegraph. Since the Great Western Railway played something of a pioneering role as far as the electric telegraph is concerned, if it had been another company that Tawell had used to make the journeys to and from the scene of the murder he might have got away with it.

Chapter Three

Railway
Financial Fraud

Whenever questions are raised concerning the thrusting entrepreneurs who pioneered the development of the major railway companies in the nineteenth century, the name of George Hudson invariably crops up. The popular perception is that he was an unscrupulous and unprincipled egomaniac who enriched himself and made paupers of others who invested their hopes and, of course, their money, in his various railway companies. The implication is that he did this through business activities which, if perhaps not always strictly illegal, were certainly unethical. Here we will outline the apparently inexorable rise of Hudson until the 'kingdom' he had created imploded and dragged him down, the fall as so often happens being far more rapid than the climb to wealth and fame.

Hudson was born in 1800 at Howsham, a small settlement between York and Malton, the fifth son of the family. His father was a tenant farmer who was moderately well off. His father and mother died before he was ten and Hudson seems to have resented John, his eldest brother, taking over as head of the family. He probably found life at home uncongenial and he left and moved to York as soon as possible.

He had no education to speak of but was remarkably confident and self-possessed. He quickly obtained employment at a draper's shop in the city. He must have made a good impression because he was only twenty when he was invited to become a partner in the business and shortly after that he married his partner's sister. The marriage was a happy one. His wife supported him by simply letting him get on with his business affairs and he therefore benefited by knowing that he had a solid domestic base for his life.

In 1827 Hudson inherited a large amount of money from a great-uncle. This episode has excited the interest of Hudson's biographers who have noted that he was never close to the man before, and indeed the suggestion has been made that he took advantage of his great-uncle's mental confusion to have the will changed so that he became the main beneficiary. The sum involved was about £30,000, a princely figure and one which was of defining importance in Hudson's life because he now had the kind of money which, if used astutely, would garner him further wealth. Now a couple of years shy of thirty, Hudson was among the richest men in York. It was about this time that he decided to become involved in the local politics of the city.

There is little doubt that many people viewed Hudson as a bad-tempered, quarrelsome, boorish and opinionated upstart, poorly educated and inexperienced. He was on the receiving end of snide comments about his humble origins and especially about the money he had suddenly come into. If such behaviour needled him, which it probably did, he was canny enough not to show it.

His response was to develop the persona of a plain-speaking, somewhat dogmatic Yorkshireman who valued common sense and hard work more highly than breeding and the sounding of his aitches. He developed very effective rhetorical skills which served him well in the rough and tumble of debate, both in the York political scene and later in the national Parliamentary political arena. He was a Conservative by party as well as being conservative by nature, and he spoke and voted consistently in opposition to proposals for social and political reform.

Money, as we all know, speaks, and while Hudson may have engendered animosity in York he was able to number himself among a group of local businessmen who set up the York Union Bank, of which he became a director. This was a useful development because this bank was to provide the finance for some of Hudson's railway schemes. The York Union Bank was associated with the prestigious Glyn's Bank of London, the chairman of which was George Carr Glyn who was keen on the promotion of new railway schemes and who proved a powerful ally to Hudson over the years.

Hudson had early learned the truth that it was who you knew and not what you knew that counted. He astutely developed relationships with some of those who would now be described as 'movers and shakers', including George and Robert Stephenson who by the mid-1830s were already prominent in railway circles for their developing skills in engineering.

Two early lines had indicated to a waiting and watching public the potential of railways for moving goods and minerals, reducing transport costs and, to a lesser extent, carrying passengers as well as producing good dividends for those investing in them. These lines were the Stockton & Darlington which started operations in 1825 and even more so the Liverpool & Manchester which opened in 1830. The success of these led to the creation of great numbers of additional schemes and proposals over the next few decades.

By no means did all of these proposals see the light of day, but those that did materialise did so in a largely unplanned and haphazard manner, and with no suggestion in the early days that the railways should be developed systematically even on a regional let alone a national basis. At this stage they were largely being built to further the interests of the business communities in the places they served, and were also often financed by the same people.

Hudson was to be a major player in the process of creating large and strong companies which came to dominate the railway industry, and also in the associated process whereby investment in railway companies was opened out to embrace a far wider range of people. These investors often had no direct business or local interest in the railways concerned. Some were simply speculators wanting quick, high returns while others were looking for a regular and reliable source of income and were often prepared to invest their life savings in order to do so.

Hudson wanted to make York into a major railway centre and in 1836 he became the largest subscriber to and chairman of a proposed York & North Midland Railway which, in conjunction with other lines in which he had an interest, would provide two possible through routes to London, albeit rather circuitous ones. York was somewhat in the doldrums at this time and Hudson reasoned that railways would provide the local economy with a much-needed fillip, not least because they would reduce the price of coal in the city and even possibly allow it to become a centre of manufacturing like the booming woollen towns in the West Riding. Obviously he saw business possibilities for himself in these developments.

The following year saw Hudson become the first Tory Lord Mayor of York, arousing envy and vilification in equal quantities as he did so. His enemies were fond of referring to him as 'the spouter of fustian' thereby calling attention to his origins as a tradesman, but Hudson was on a roll and quite prepared to mix it verbally with any or all of his enemies. In fact his public attacks on political enemies were scurrilous even by the standards of the time, and he was happy to make his political differences personal ones as well.

He surrounded himself with a clique of toadies and placemen who, because they owed their positions to his patronage, almost fell over themselves to do whatever he wanted them to do. There is an expression to the effect that the higher the monkey climbs the tree, the more it shows its bottom. His enemies would have been mindful of this charming old adage. Doubtless Hudson was as well, but at this time in his burgeoning career he probably thought he was fireproof.

Hudson made quite a splash as Lord Mayor and the local Tories wanted him to continue. This was against the rules because his term as an alderman had run out and only aldermen were eligible to be considered for the role of Lord Mayor. They bent the rules by appointing him as an alderman again, whereupon he was quickly re-elected as Lord Mayor. This caused a furore among his opponents and an enquiry declared that this action was illegal. However, the enquiry was so long-winded that Hudson decided to brazen it out and had actually finished his second term as Lord Mayor before it was published. By that time he could not have cared less anyway. This somewhat shady episode tells us something about the man and his essential pragmatism.

The York & North Midland Railway proved to be a great success but it is interesting to note that at the company's annual shareholders' meeting in 1840 some of those present raised concerns about the company's book-keeping methods. They were in a minority because most shareholders were highly gratified by the large dividend which Hudson had announced, but they did suggest that professional auditors should be appointed to scrutinise the accounts. Hudson contemptuously swept this proposal aside by telling them that the directors of the company on their behalf had access whenever required to the company's books and they were perfectly satisfied with the way things were being done. Although the matter was dropped, could it be that a few shareholders knew or at least suspected that Hudson may have been cooking the books?

Hudson's career as a railway entrepreneur was striding forward as he gained important roles in many new companies that were being set-up. For example, the North Midland Railway Company was having financial problems and Hudson offered to bale it out. The price of this was a place for Hudson on the board of directors with complete autonomy on management and financial matters. He had the Midas touch; no sooner was he at the helm of the North Midland than the shares of the company began to rise impressively. The man had vision, no one can argue with that.

Probably his most inspirational move ever was to mastermind the merger of four companies into the Midland Railway with himself as its chairman. This occurred in 1844 and was the first of many such amalgamations and consolidations over the next decades, although these were carried out by other 'railway barons'. Historians generally consider these mergers to have had a beneficial economic effect and that they were necessary. Hudson should be given the credit for having the foresight to recognise that big was beautiful in railway terms at the time, although it is unlikely that his primary motivation was the long-term welfare of Britain's developing railway system.

The creation of the Midland Railway meant that Hudson now had under his control a network based on Derby with lines that stretched as far away as Rugby, Birmingham, Bristol and York. He had considerable influence in many other companies. There were lots of people now who treated him with awe and respect but his visible success only confirmed other people's undying enmity towards him. One of his biographers terms him 'The Railway King' and likened him to Cardinal Wolsey who was similarly of relatively humble origins as well as blustering, bullying, exceptionally able, ambitious, unscrupulous and egotistical. Like Wolsey, Hudson was eventually to fly too near the sun.

Hudson was not a railwayman, an engineer nor an economist – he was first and foremost a businessman, a financial wheeler-dealer with very considerable talent in the role he played. It was his good fortune and ultimately his fate to be around when the railway system was booming and rich pickings were available for such a bold and ruthless entrepreneur. Had some other type of business enterprise come on the scene offering better prospects than the railways, we can be pretty sure that he would have thrown himself into it without turning a hair. Until the 'Credit Crunch' of 2008-9 he would probably have been a property developer or hedge fund manager. During the two world wars he would have been a profiteer in munitions or essential commodities in short supply and would have made a mint for himself.

In 1845 Hudson contested a by-election and won the Sunderland seat for the Conservatives. This was not just a personal triumph for Hudson but, pragmatically, he knew that being an MP would make it easier for him to fight those who were advocating closer regulation of the railways in the public interest.

In the mid-1840s the so-called 'Railway Mania' was in full swing and Parliament was being presented with a flood of railway schemes all seeking legislative approval. In 1846 Parliament passed no fewer than 219 Acts authorising the building of 4,500 miles of new railways with a capital of over £132 million. Such had been the success of some railways in consistently returning high dividends to shareholders that it was not difficult to raise capital – from businessmen who believed that the proposed line might benefit their enterprises, from professional speculators out to make a quick killing and from genuine small investors looking for a nest egg.

In some cases, however, crooks simply produced a company prospectus and with honeyed words about the golden prospects that could be had invited people to buy shares in lines for which they had no intention of seeking parliamentary approval let alone of actually building. When they had obtained what they considered to be sufficient sums of money by such fraudulent practices, the slippery promoters would simply cut and run only to pop up somewhere else a year or two later doing the same thing.

It was in 1846 to 1847 that Hudson's prestige and power were probably at their apogee. His town house was a sumptuous mansion in Regent's Park and there he hobnobbed with the so-called greatest in the land – the leading politicians, scientists and thinkers and influential landowners up to and including the aged and irascible Duke of Wellington. Many of these people privately sneered at Hudson for his lack of breeding, but it had become prudent to keep such feelings private. It was by no means uncommon for the highest born to fawn around him and ask his advice or practical assistance with their business affairs, especially if they concerned railways. This must have gratified his ego enormously, but for the Hudsons of this world a pratfall is never far away.

Late in 1847 he found himself in hot water when the Leeds & Bradford Railway Company was taken over by the Midland. This takeover was the handiwork of Hudson who stood to gain because he was chairman of the two companies and had a substantial holding of shares in both. His enemies, and he had them even among the shareholders of the Midland, joyfully rounded on what they saw as a prime example of sharp practice and the issue was raised at the shareholders' meeting. This meeting was extremely stormy and Hudson was unusually flustered. He lost his temper and told the dissidents – in language that would have done credit to a drunken bargee – that as long as his efforts brought them rich dividends they had no right to complain about the methods he employed in order to obtain those dividends. He had a point but so, of course, did they.

It began to go downhill for Hudson from then on. Almost imperceptibly at first but developing a momentum of their own were signs that the previous seemingly impregnable bastions of Hudson Castle were developing hairline fractures. Progressively these began expanding into cracks and fissures. Hudson had been asked to bail out the absolutely hopeless Eastern Counties Railway, an opportunity which he seized eagerly. This would have been a challenge for anyone, but when as chairman he received an avalanche of complaints about the habitual lateness of the trains being run by this company his response was that since many of the trains ran early then their timings effectively cancelled out those that ran late!

This was extremely feeble stuff from someone whose previous responses to criticism had been supremely bullish and confident, and it was taken by his enemies as evidence that he was beginning to lose his grip. For many years Hudson had been assiduously attacked by hostile satirical cartoonists as a Tory with unacceptably right-wing views or as little more than a loud-mouthed and hectoring bully, albeit a man with very considerable power. Now he was being portrayed as something of a buffoon out of control, careering along being propelled by his own trains!

For the first time, shareholders were no longer necessarily hanging on his every word nor supporting his suggestions without question. His persuasiveness was starting to run out of steam. It is significant that in 1848 Hudson made the last two additions to the bulging portfolio of the railway companies he controlled or in which he had a major say.

In 1849 his old friend George Stephenson died. They had worked closely for many years but Stephenson had of late distanced himself somewhat from Hudson over concerns about some of his business methods. About this time Hudson fell ill for almost the first time in his life. His excessive work output was probably a major factor but he ate and drank to excess as well. It became increasingly evident that some of his speeches in the House of Commons were made under the influence of drink. This probably helps to explain why on occasions they were either belligerent, bafflingly incoherent, or both!

In 1849 the hitherto unknown Arthur Smith produced a pamphlet with the less than riveting and seemingly innocuous title *The Bubble of the Age or the Fallacies of Railway Investment, Railway Accounts and Railway Dividends.* It proved to be a best-seller. In it Smith called into question the accountancy methods and dividend and interest practices of Britain's railway companies in general. However, he pointed to the York & North Midland and Eastern Counties Railway companies in particular. In making the specific allegation that they paid dividends out of capital rather than revenue, Smith was clearly implying that the chairman of these companies was guilty of improper business practices. Hudson was not amused. Smith's pamphlet was the harbinger of further horrors to come.

The financial downturn in the late 1840s brought with it a sharp decline in railway profits and dividends, from which Hudson's companies were not immune. Previously many of those who had investments in his companies had sat back expecting continuing rich returns courtesy of Hudson's entrepreneurial skills. Truly he had been the goose that laid the golden eggs. Now that the eggs were no longer golden but merely lion-stamped, many of these people rounded on him and joined the chorus that claimed that he was personally to blame for the downward trend in their investments.

It was but a short step from criticising his managerial abilities to questioning the integrity of his business methods as well. For his part Hudson pointed to the general financial downturn and also to his record of success on their behalf in an attempt to assure restive shareholders that the good times would return if they stuck with him.

At the 1849 annual shareholders meeting of the York, Newcastle & Berwick Railway Company, another in Hudson's portfolio, up jumped a shareholder by the name of Robert Prance. He happened to be a member of the London Stock Exchange and was known to be well versed in matters of high finance. The question he put, which he assured fellow shareholders was based on painstaking research, turned out to be an accusation that Hudson was guilty of what would now be termed 'insider dealing' and that he had made substantial profits in the shares of another of his railway companies by drawing on the funds of the York, Newcastle & Berwick Railway, doing so at the expense of the company's shareholders.

Up to this time, the meeting had been nothing other than routine but Prance's intervention absolutely galvanised those present. Everyone, Hudson's friends and foes alike, were on tenterhooks waiting to see how Hudson handled his response. When he got up to speak all his customary bombast had evaporated. He looked crestfallen and sounded confused and unconvincing. He told the meeting that without the books in front of him he could not tell who was responsible, if indeed there had been any wrongdoing, but he would instigate an immediate investigation and if a case was proven, he would not only discipline those involved but personally recompense any shareholders who had suffered losses.

This stunned his audience as being such a contrast to his customary ebulliently confident manner. Worse was to follow. Hudson then stood speechless and motionless for probably no more than a few seconds but in a time-lapse which must have seemed like an eternity to his audience and, most of all, to him. He then falteringly blurted out that he had indeed exploited his position to buy shares cheaply and sell them on very profitably. He apologised and stated that he was prepared to take the shares back and make a full refund to anyone in the meeting. After this the meeting was in uproar and Prance's motion that a committee should investigate the issue gained the backing of the meeting.

A few days later Hudson was due to preside at the annual shareholders' meeting of the Eastern Counties Railway, but foreseeing a rough ride he gave his apologies. This was seen by those at the meeting as tantamount to an admission of fraudulent practice and the meeting decided that a committee should be established to look into the growing concerns about Hudson's financial probity. Even in the apparently solid redoubt of Hudson's financial and managerial activities – the Midland Railway – questions began to be asked, and when a majority of shareholders requested a meeting with him, if only to assure them that there were no unanswered questions, Hudson resigned his chairmanship.

It was now coming thick and fast. The commission that resulted from Prance's efforts had published its report and confirmed that Hudson had been involved in share dealing contrary to company law. He had fixed the price of shares in the Great North of England Railway which he then sold to the York, Newcastle & Berwick. He had also breached company law by having financial involvement with two companies which had been engaged in business negotiations with each other. Now many who had previously clung to Hudson's coat-tails hastily abandoned him while simultaneously trying to drop him in it. When one such turncoat revealed that Hudson had told him to alter some accounts to make them more acceptable to the shareholders of one of his companies, the 'Railway King' was sunk.

When the shareholders of the Eastern Counties Railway issued their report, Hudson had little option but to appear before them. By now he was a broken man, humbly, even cringingly explaining that he had indeed paid dividends out of capital in an attempt to attract further investment and by way of excuse saying that the amounts concerned were not great, although he would not or could not specify exactly how much was involved. He asked for various other financial irregularities to be taken into account.

George Hudson in his prime.

In May 1849 Hudson was heartbroken when the body of his beloved brother-in-law was hauled out of the river Ouse at York. He had committed suicide as the result of the investigations into Hudson's financial dealings which in turn had implicated him. Soon afterwards Hudson appeared in the House of Commons to answer a number of questions about his financial affairs. Gone was all his previous self-confidence, and the physically and mentally shrunken man's statement was received with a stony silence.

A few days later the shareholders' meeting of the York & North Midland Railway learned how the company funds had been tapped for electoral expenses and also how Hudson had used company funds to build a private station close to his country home at Londesborough Park. He resigned with immediate effect as a flood of other damaging accusations and allegations came at him from every angle.

Either voluntarily or under duress he had to make a series of payments to various companies and individuals. It was only the fact that he was an MP that meant that he was not arrested for debt. Wisely he spent much of his later years living abroad, but by then he was in greatly straitened circumstances. He was in London on 11 December 1870 when he had a heart attack and he died shortly afterwards. When his will was read he had assets of just £200 – not much for the 'Railway King'.

OFF THE RAIL.

George Hudson depicted coming off the rails. Caricaturists often showed him as a symbolic locomotive with a crown for a chimney.

Hudson broke the law and he breached business ethics, but there were many people who had been aware of this and had heard or seen no evil as long as the dividends kept rolling in. They then hypocritically and sanctimoniously rounded on the man when he was no longer coming up with the goods. A scapegoat was needed and Hudson fitted the bill. He was by no means unique in the history of capitalism as a businessman who accumulated and wielded wealth and power while not being too fussy about the methods he employed to do so. Those who benefited were not too fussy either.

The 'Railway Mania' period was a financial bubble, and like other bubbles it was rooted in the 'get-rich-quick' ethos. Hudson did get rich quickly, but in doing so he enriched many others along the way. The bubble, however, was bound to burst and inevitably Hudson was undone when that happened.

The earlier railway companies with which Hudson was associated were nearly all set-up as the result of their own specific private Acts of Parliament, which laid out in considerable detail the powers and responsibilities of their directors and of the chairman. In 1845 the alliterative Companies Clauses Consolidation Act codified practice on such matters as the role of directors and the act was applied to all new statutory companies. Hudson could therefore never have said that he was unaware of his legal obligations and responsibilities.

Research has identified five definite cases where Hudson embezzled money from one or other of the railway companies of which he was the chairman, and has highlighted up to eight occasions when Hudson most certainly acted in breach of his responsibilities as a director. He was involved in the falsification of the accounts of several of his companies, in particular the Eastern Counties. Although one of his biographers says that Hudson 'raised creative accounting to an art form'[1] he always argued that everything he did was intended to benefit the railway companies which he controlled. His ego and his compulsive desire for wealth and power meant that, like many other entrepreneurs, he found it hard to differentiate between what was simply in his own interests and that which might have – or actually did – benefit other people. Significantly Hudson was never prosecuted in a criminal court.

Other later buccaneering entrepreneurs such as Horatio Bottomley, Robert Maxwell and John Dolorean, for example, could also do no wrong when the force was with them but they too were eventually caught out. When that happened those people, who only the previous day had been singing their praises and turning a blind eye to their business practices, started trilling a very different song.

There are parallels to be drawn between Hudson and those bankers and other supposed financial high-flyers whose self-seeking activities came to light in the 'credit crunch'. The reality is that most people knew that their activities, if not actually illegal, were fuelling a speculative boom which would have disastrous effects when it eventually collapsed. One day such people had the Midas touch. The next day, when the inevitable collapse had happened, the bankers found themselves being almost universally excoriated for their 'greed'.

William Gladstone, a leading figure on the British political scene in the second half of the nineteenth century, ruminated on Hudson's fall from grace while exhibiting some talent as a poetaster. There was much that he admired about Hudson's energy and vision but he also knew about the man's sharp practice and he circulated friends with a little verse to that effect. Hudson, he said:

> ... bamboozled the mob; he bamboozled the quality;
> He led both through the quagmire of gross immorality.[2]

With some vehemence Gladstone went on – rightly – to condemn the pious self-righteousness of those who apparently only discovered the man's ethical shortcomings once he could no longer serve them up their unearned income.

The career of Hudson, his rise and fall, was the product of an economic and social system undergoing a particularly dynamic and volatile period in its evolution. The 'Railway Mania' encouraged human greed and fed off human gullibility. The railway promoters and managers of the nineteenth century were not noted for their moral scruples. They operated in a dog-eat-dog world and those who were successful – as Hudson was for many years – needed to be ahead of the field in the extent to which they were far-sighted, quick-thinking, ruthless, determined and decisive. If it is felt necessary to judge Hudson, it can only be within the context of the circumstances that produced him.

The Redpath Frauds

One of the most spectacular examples in the nineteenth century of fraud associated with the railways was the case of Leopold Redpath. In August 1856 Edmund Dennison, the chairman of the Great Northern Railway, had addressed a meeting of shareholders in a forthright, even bullish, fashion. Among other things he stated his utmost confidence in the honesty and probity of the company's employees. In fact he was being somewhat economical with the truth, which was that a couple of years earlier some discrepancies had been discovered in the company's books.

They related to differences, apparently not huge ones, between the amounts paid in dividends and the amount due to be paid on the stock registered. The company's officer in charge of the share registration department was a lawyer by the name of Clerk who knew virtually nothing about this aspect of the company's work. He was due to retire and before he did so he stated that he was confident that the matter could be safely left in the hands of his successor who just happened to be the aforementioned Redpath.

In fact Redpath had basically been doing Clerk's job under the guise of helping him out and had become indispensable. He saw to it that he kept his knowledge of the department's work to himself. He had arrived at the Great Northern with glowing references. These, in fact, were forged. Redpath, who had once been declared bankrupt, had in fact left his previous employment under a cloud. Not to put too fine a point on it he had had his fingers in the till.

So we have Leopold Redpath in charge of the entire GNR's stock and share register while he was creating fraudulent stocks and printing numbered stock certificates which were not included in the company's books but were being sold through stockbrokers to eager investors. He sold so much bogus scrip that the company was paying out increasingly large amounts of money as dividends when it had never received the capital used to buy the shares in the first place. One of his subordinates had pointed out some discrepancies.

Redpath thanked him for his vigilance and promised that he would carry out an investigation. Understandably this investigation proceeded extremely slowly, but suspicion was building up that something fishy was going on, and at the next shareholder's meeting Dennison announced to an enraged audience that because an employee had been selling forged shares the state of the company finances meant that there would be no dividends for that half-year.

When the inevitable happened and the police called at his home with a request that they help them with their enquiries Redpath was consuming a large cooked breakfast as though he had not a care in the world. He had the sense to co-operate fully with the process of the law. His character puzzled the authorities. They expected such a big-time swindler to be brash and ostentatious. Instead he was charming, modest and almost self-effacing. His only extravagance was the ownership of two houses, one in London and one in what was once described as 'the Surrey stockbroker belt', and the throwing of fine dinner parties at which many of society's so-called elite would appear. Most of his ill-gotten gains he gave away to charity! People simply could not understand why a swindler should take such risks in order to benefit those less fortunate than himself.

However, his charitable works cut no ice with the court when he appeared at the Old Bailey in 1857. Redpath was sentenced to transportation for life and his assets, to the tune of £25,000 – then a very considerable sum – were sequestered and paid to the Great Northern as partial compensation for the loss they had incurred, a far greater sum estimated at £250,000. What is remarkable is that the frauds were so simple and blatant that a few minutes inspection of the GNR's register of stocks at any time between 1848 and 1856 would have revealed that fraud was taking place. It is small wonder then that Redpath had kept his cards, or rather the GNR books, so close to his chest and for so long.

The Redpath affair severely shook public confidence in the financial management of the railway companies in general and the Great Northern in particular. A concomitant of this was the emergence of the professional accountant as a replacement for the willing, but often blatantly ignorant, amateur auditor of company accounts. Over the years many railway employees

One of the courts in the Old Bailey. How many dramatic courtroom scenes have taken place in these surroundings?

found ways to embezzle the companies they worked for but their activities were small beer compared with those of Hudson and Redpath.

Why Not Travel Free?

A consistent theme throughout the history of railway crime has been that of fare evasion. The Regulation of Railways Act of 1840 made travelling on the railway without a ticket a criminal offence. Additionally, railway companies could sue passengers in civil courts to recover the cost of the fares concerned. As early as 1905 at least one railway company displayed posters 'naming and shaming' passengers who had been successfully prosecuted for fare evasion. Some of the Train Operating Companies on the UK's current scandalously denationalised railway 'system' have employed similar methods in recent years. Considerable ingenuity has been exercised by travellers in their attempts to avoid the cost of buying the appropriate ticket.

In the 1860s a most enterprising woman devised her own means of travelling around the British railway system largely free of charge. Her name seems to have been Nell and her first escapade was to be found apparently unconscious on a train at Strood in north Kent. A doctor pronounced her dead and she was taken to the morgue whereupon she amazed everyone by sitting up and gazing around in confusion. The bemused authorities then moved her to the workhouse but she had only been there a few minutes when she brought tears to their eyes by saying that she had been on her way to see her brother but had been drugged and robbed on the train. She was now penniless – but did not remain so for long. The kind-hearted stationmaster heard this tale of woe and promptly issued her with a complementary ticket and gave her £5 from his own pocket.

Perhaps encouraged by her success as an actress and confidence-trickster, she later turned up pulling the same stunt and spinning a similar yarn at New Street station, Birmingham, at Shrewsbury and at Paddington. The latter was one stunt too many. The Great Western Railway police had heard about her and she was arrested. She served a three-month custodial sentence. It is amazing that she was able to feign death successfully and to pass examination by doctors so many times. Those privy to these actions agreed that she might have made a fortune on the stage.

Back in the 1890s a busker left a train carrying what was clearly a full-size harp, presumably his stock-in-trade, covered in green baize. Nothing wrong with that, you might say. An alert railway policeman thought that the man was making rather heavy weather of carrying the instrument. When the musician approached the barrier proffering the correct ticket for his journey, the officer decided to stop and question him, and in doing so discovered that the musician's daughter, very small for her age but old enough to require a ticket, was huddling inside the package. The busker had not paid for her.

A group of young men travelling to Reading for the races did not bother to buy tickets but displayed some enterprise by jumping off at Reading while the train was slowing to a halt approaching the platform. Then they pretended to be ticket collectors and accosted passengers as they alighted from the train, demanding that they surrender their tickets. They did this brazenly enough to harvest more than enough tickets for all of them and then surrendered them as they passed through the barriers, leaving a sorry gaggle of bemused passengers to explain why they were without tickets. It all goes to show that if you have enough front, you can get away with anything.

In the early days of the railways a few enterprising characters tried forging their own railway tickets, not always successfully. It is said that nature abhors a vacuum and the railway industry owes an enormous debt of gratitude to Thomas Edmondson (1792–1851) who, around 1840, successfully filled a vacuum by developing a ticketing system which was very widely adopted, both at home and abroad. His invention rendered the forgery of railway tickets much more difficult.

Many early 'authorities to travel' had consisted of forms in which the relevant details were filled in by hand and were easy to forge. Edmondson was a clerk in the booking office of a wayside station on the Newcastle &

Carlisle Railway. He invented a system of pre-printed card tickets containing all the necessary details of each journey booked. Each ticket had its own unique sequential number, distinguishing colours could be used for different classes or types of travel and each ticket was stamped with the relevant date by a machine into which the ticket was inserted. The ticket acted as a receipt which clearly denoted the journey involved and the numbering of each ticket assisted in the process of bookkeeping. These tickets remained in general use until well into the 1960s and their last use by British Railways was in 1990.

In 1875 a gentleman travelling on the Midland Railway from Leicester to St Pancras was arrested at Kentish Town when he was unable to produce a ticket. The staff concerned must have been somewhat heavy-handed and as a result the traveller hit one of them. Upon arrival at the police station the ticket, which the passenger had vehemently claimed he had bought in the normal way, was found. Cleared of the accusation of fare evasion, the focus then turned to the excessive use of force by the railwaymen involved and the magistrates chastised the Midland for employing people who used violence so freely.

In American hobo folklore there are all sorts of stories of people bumming free journeys by 'riding the rods', these being part of the appendages to be found under boxcars. This hair-raising way of avoiding the expense of a ticket was rare but not unknown in Britain. In the late nineteenth century there were a few cases, such as the man who had managed to travel under a carriage hanging on to its brake gear all the way from Holyhead to Chester, and another who did a similarly hazardous and uncomfortable trip from Euston to Rugby, in both cases on the London & North Western Railway.

In 1938 a passenger was prosecuted for riding on the roof of an overnight train to Scotland. He had been carousing with friends and was more than a little drunk before deciding to hitch a free ride. He quickly sobered up once he realised what a hazardous situation he had got himself into and indeed he almost fell off several times when the carriage gave a sudden lurch. Suitably chastened, he made his way down to the platform at the first stop only to face a hostile reception from station staff and the railway police. He was fined.

The printing of tickets by passengers is a fine example of self-help but one not approved of by the railway authorities. One man produced very high-quality tickets in the 1930s but was found out after the Second World War when he submitted a ticket bearing the company name 'LNER' when the railways had just been nationalised. Counterfeit and foreign coins have been used in ticket machines but technology has gradually reduced the possibilities of this kind of fraud. Providing the wrong name and address is also a criminal act. Railway-users have been prosecuted for doing so.

1   Beaumont, R. *The Railway King*, p.255.
2   Quoted in Bailey, B. George Hudson, *The Rise and Fall of the Railway King*, p.153.

CHAPTER FOUR

MURDER ON THE LINE
1900-2000

A Murder on the train up to Town

It was just after midday on a January morning in 1901 when Mrs Rhoda King entered a third-class compartment of a train of the London & South Western Railway at the main station in Southampton. The train was bound for London Waterloo. It was due to stop only at Eastleigh, Winchester and at Vauxhall which was just short of Waterloo, and where all the passengers' tickets were inspected. Vauxhall was ideal for Rhoda because it was much closer to Battersea – where she was going to visit her poorly sister – than Waterloo was.

Rhoda had a husband and children but she was a strong-minded sort and quite used to travelling long distances on her own at a time when some women at least were becoming more assertive and independent. She left Southampton as the only occupant of the compartment. Such single occupancy was viewed by most travellers with mixed feelings. Many of them enjoyed being on their own and they resented anyone else entering the compartment and intruding on their 'territory'.

Many passengers, however, and not only women, were more unhappy about sharing a single compartment with just one other male stranger. He might make unwanted advances, or worse. He might be intent on robbery. He might simply be an incredible bore who would relentlessly inflict his life story on the captive audience so conveniently provided by the compartment type of carriage. If two or more passengers entered the compartment then these scenarios were immediately rendered much less likely.

Soon after leaving Southampton the train pulled into Eastleigh where a giant of a young fellow joined Rhoda. He gave her a friendly enough nod and she smiled back, rather admiring his height and his powerful build. He looked quite a man. She felt inclined to engage him in conversation but did not want to appear too forward. The opportunity to follow up their brief salutation passed and each remained silent as the train proceeded on its way. It was not far to Winchester, where a third person entered the compartment. This was a Mr William Pearson who looked just like a well-set-up farmer, which is not surprising because that is exactly what he was. He was clearly worth a bob or two and the young man's eyes must have lit up.

Now our young man who had got in at Eastleigh went by the name of George Parker, and while there was much about his appearance that attracted women he was a thoroughly bad lot. He was twenty-three and had managed to cram a fair amount of skulduggery into his short life. He had been in the army but had been dishonourably discharged after a brief career punctuated by various unacceptable misdemeanours. He was wanted by the police in connection with an act of theft at the Lyceum Theatre in London's West End where he had worked.

Now he was returning to London after enjoying several days of robust rumpy pumpy with an older married woman from the Eastleigh district. She had been at the station to see him off and observers were surprised by just how passionate the couple's embraces had been. This activity, of course, unlike the others, was not a disciplinary matter nor was it punishable by the law, but it does suggest that Parker was a young man who took his chances where he could find them.

He was chancing it now, being on the train with a ticket which authorised him to travel only as far as Winchester. For him this was a mere technicality. Living life according to his own standards – to the full – he was permanently strapped for cash. He was hanging around trains looking for someone to rob, and by doing so hoping to get at least short-term surcease from his money problems. He had bought a revolver with robbery in mind.

The three passengers sat in the compartment apparently studiously ignoring each other. In fact Rhoda kept sneaking admiring glances at the good-looking Parker. He in turn was eyeing up Pearson and had come to the conclusion that he looked just the kind of person who was worth robbing. Pearson for his part looked at no one in particular. He dozed and sporadically gazed out of the window.

Parker decided that he would rob the rustic-looking gentleman sitting opposite. If he resisted, then he would have to be shot and killed. Dead men tell no tales. Since dead women also tell no tales, he would have to do the same to the woman. This was a shame because he had spotted her eyeing him up and rather felt that he would like to take the acquaintance further. She did not look as if she was carrying much money though.

Parker noted that the train was passing Surbiton and that the deed would have to be done soon or not at all. As the train was approaching Clapham

Junction Parker pulled out his gun and with no more ado shot Pearson, killing him instantly. Next he fired at Rhoda, winging her on her face, and then hurled the pistol out of the window at Nine Elms as the train was slowing for the Vauxhall stop.

He quickly rifled through Pearson's pockets. Even before the train had drawn to a halt Parker had leapt out onto the platform, rushed to the barrier, shoved the ticket which he had removed from Pearson's pocket into the ticket inspector's face, and before the latter had recovered from the sudden whirlwind that overwhelmed him Parker was running full tilt down the ramp to the street level.

By this time, Rhoda, bleeding profusely but not seriously injured, had raised the alarm. Various he-men took off in hot pursuit of the rapidly retreating Parker who tried to hide, but his pursuers quickly found, seized and overwhelmed him. Parker appeared at the Old Bailey, was found guilty of murder and executed at Wandsworth Prison on 19 March 1901.

From a distance of more than a century, one is left pondering over the essential stupidity of Parker. Riding around on trains with no intention of paying the full fare was one thing but thinking that he could get away with robbery and commit murder on a train was completely different. However, this is a kind of myopic arrogance often found among murderers who convince themselves that they are so clever that they are somehow immune from the fate of ordinary individuals.

Murdering for Coal

Birmingham is one of those places that contradict the admittedly rather glib and simplistic generalisation that rapid urban and industrial growth in Britain was a result of the coming of the railways. Places such as Middlesborough, Crewe, Barrow-in-Furness and Springburn in Glasgow come readily to mind in support of this assertion. Birmingham, however, was the hub of England's canal system and a leading industrial centre from the eighteenth century well before the coming of the railways. It went on to become a major centre of the railway system.

A prime contender for the title of least-loved station in Britain is Birmingham New Street. East of New Street and visible on the north side of the line from trains leaving Birmingham for such places as Leicester, Stansted Airport, Derby, Sheffield, Coventry and London Euston is a grand building standing in glorious isolation in distinctly dystopian surroundings. This is the former Curzon Street station, the original terminus of the London & Birmingham Railway.

It opened in 1839 and was designed by Philip Hardwick as a counterpart to his Euston station in London fronted by the famous Doric Arch. It has somehow managed to evade the modernising barbarians who did for the whole of the old Euston, good bits and bad. Curzon Street closed to regular passenger traffic when the more convenient New Street was opened in 1854. It became part of a large railway goods depot being used as offices until 1968.

Coal has been described as 'black gold', and while actually having more utility than gold it is nevertheless generally regarded as less valuable. In the age when it was the only major source of domestic heating it was frequently stolen – sometimes by opportunist individuals who wanted to cut down on their fuel bills but also by professional thieves who found a ready sale for cheap coal on the black market – no pun intended.

In 1901 coal had been disappearing from wagons in coal merchants' sidings at Curzon Street. Not the odd lump but entire sacks. This is the reason why a detective officer in the London & North Western Railway's police force was patrolling on the evening of 10 August. His name was Hibbs. He knew the area well and realised that he was almost certainly up against professionals because the thieves had so far evaded all attempts by the police to catch them. Hibbs was well aware of the danger that went with his solitary patrol but he was experienced and had a whistle which he hoped would bring quick assistance if needed.

He spotted three men dragging sacks of coal out of the depot and called on them to stop. They abandoned the sacks and ran off along the nearby canal with Hibbs in hot pursuit. Realising that he was on his own, they turned to face him. Hibbs drew his truncheon as all three of the thieves went for him. It was a brave action but it proved to be an unwise one. It was never a fair fight and he was knocked down and rendered unconscious by a heavy blow to the back of the head. Callously they then picked him up as if he was no more than a bundle of rubbish and threw him into the canal where he drowned.

The Coroner's Court returned a verdict of 'wilful murder by persons unknown'. The London & North Western Railway offered a reward of £100 for information leading to the conviction of those responsible. The police already had three young local men in custody but they needed more evidence. Some of the witnesses who had come forward had complained of anonymous threats and clearly felt intimidated. Would they be prepared to testify in court? The civil police felt sure that these were the three men responsible but the evidence was largely circumstantial and would be unlikely to stand up in court.

The railway police, however, were prepared to take the risk, understandably anxious not to allow the murder of one of their number to go unpunished. To their chagrin, however, the case against the men was conditionally discharged on the grounds of insufficient evidence. The case remains unsolved to this day.

Found: Body in a Tunnel

The original Merstham Tunnel was built for the London, Brighton & South Coast Railway in 1839. A new tunnel was built in 1899 alongside and it was in this later tunnel that a gang of track workers made a gruesome discovery around 11p.m. on Sunday 24 September 1905.

The men were doing routine maintenance work on the track by the fitful light of oil lamps which cast weird shadows on the sooty walls of the tunnel. It was dangerous and uncongenial work but it had to be done, and the fact that there were fewer trains about at this time of the evening did at least reduce the ever-present fear of all platelayers and gangers which was, of course, that of being run down by a fast-moving train, always a possibility even with vigilant lookouts.

In charge of the gang was William Peacock, who was moving somewhat ahead of the rest of the men when he discovered something lying by the side of the track. As he moved nearer he realised to his horror that it was the badly mutilated body of a woman. One leg had been severed cleanly, the face was badly knocked about and bloodied and the left arm brutally crushed. The stationmaster at Merstham was immediately informed as were the police. The body was removed and temporarily housed at the Feathers Hotel where an inquest would take place. There was nothing on or around the corpse which gave any clue to its identity.

The original theory was that the woman had committed suicide but foul play could not be ruled out. Large numbers of people were interviewed by the police, some of them giving answers which were unsatisfactory and needed to be checked out. This took several days and the police acknowledged that they were no nearer identifying the woman. Then, out of the blue, a man came forward asking to be allowed to view the body. This was an unusual request, and given that there were many odd people about the police took a lot of persuading before acceding.

Obviously it was not a pretty sight but the man told them that it was the remains of his sister Mary Sophia Money. She had been just twenty-two years old, was unmarried and had worked in a dairy in a clerical capacity. She lived at Lavender Hill in south-east London. She was small, although well-built and altogether an attractive young woman. Men would have wished to get to know her but she certainly did not seem to have a regular 'admirer'. Her brother could not furnish any reason why she might have committed suicide.

What began to militate against the suicide theory was that she had clearly been gagged. It was hard to believe that someone contemplating suicide would gag themselves so as not to make any noise. Examination of where the body was found suggested that she had been thrown from the train and had hit the tunnel wall where there were marks as if she had slid down the tunnel-side, her fingers gouging out the soot. As she slid down the wall it was likely that one of her legs fell over the rail and was severed when the wheels went over it.

Enquiries revealed that on the day in question Mary had told a friend that she was going out for a short while but she never returned. At about 7p.m. she had gone into her local sweet shop as she did regularly on Wednesdays and Sundays. She had chatted briefly and told the shopkeeper that she was going to Victoria. Evidently Mary had told two different stories about what she meant to do and the police concluded that the deception was intentional and that she was going to a clandestine meeting with a person unknown at a destination equally unknown.

She certainly did go to Victoria because a ticket collector recognised her from a photograph. What seemed odd was that she was not dressed for walking or for going any great distance. What then had she been doing on a train destined for Brighton? Did she meet up with a paramour unknown to her family? Did she get on the Brighton train with this man and why? What happened between the couple in what was presumably an otherwise empty compartment? Did he make sexual advances which were rejected whereupon he lost his temper and threw her out of the train in a fit of pique? Questions, questions, but no answers.

It did emerge that a signalman on duty watched a train go past that day and saw what he thought was a struggle taking place in one of the compartments but even this was not much help. The murderer of Mary Sophia Money was never found.

Murder on the North Eastern Railway

In the age of relative innocence that was Britain in the years leading up to the First World War, it was a common practice for clerical workers to travel around on public transport carrying bags containing the wages of the employees of the companies they worked for. Sometimes they carried amounts that by today's values would be tens of thousands of pounds.

On 10 March 1910 John Nisbet, who lived in Heaton Road on the northeast side of Newcastle-upon-Tyne, was at the city's Central station carrying a leather bag containing £370 9s 6d for the workers of the Stobswood Colliery Company. He was on his fortnightly trip from the colliery to Newcastle with a company cheque which he had cashed at Lloyd's Bank. This involved a return journey on the North Eastern Railway from Stannington station, the closest station to the pit where he worked. Although the line on which the train ran was a main line, this particular train was a humble and lightly used

Newcastle central station is by some distance the largest nineteenth-century building in the city. Much of it is the work of John Dobson, who designed many of Newcastle's finest buildings of that time.

stopping train calling at all stations to Alnmouth, where it terminated. Such trains often had average speeds of little more than twenty miles per hour.

Nisbet, who was well known, was seen by a number of people at Newcastle Central station before he caught the stopping train back to Stannington. They included two other cashiers working for colliery companies who were engaged in the same duties as himself. These witnesses saw Nisbet walking the platform with a man called Dickman with whom he got into a compartment towards the front of the train. Dickman was wearing a light-coloured overcoat.

Nisbet was an uxorious husband and it was the regular practice for his wife to come to Heaton station to meet the train. It usually halted there for a few minutes, during which time he lowered the carriage window and the couple then perhaps proceeded to whisper sweet nothings to each other. On this occasion the train halted only briefly and she just had time to note that another passenger was sharing her husband's compartment. He was wearing a light-coloured overcoat but his collar was raised and it was impossible for her to tell whether she knew him.

At Stannington the two other cashiers alighted from the train, one of them giving a nod to Nisbet as he passed the compartment in which he was travelling. He noted a man sharing Nisbet's compartment. He wore a light-coloured overcoat. If the cashier thought it odd that Nisbet was apparently making no effort to leave the train himself he said nothing and had soon forgotten the matter.

The train puffed wearily on its way calling a few minutes later at Morpeth. There were few passengers alighting but one who did handed the ticket collector half of a return ticket from Newcastle to Stannington and he proffered the excess fare. It was our man in the light-coloured overcoat. Eventually the train steamed into Alnmouth where the practice was for a porter to examine all the compartments before the train was prepared for its return trip. He opened a compartment in the leading coach and then staggered back, vomiting violently.

The body of a man was lying spread-eagled and face downwards on the floor in a pool of blood. Clearly a murder had taken place but it was also immediately evident that a violent struggle had also occurred. An initial examination by the local police, quite excited because they could not remember the last time they had had to deal with a murder, showed that the man had been shot five times in the head. Two bullets were still lodged in the victim's skull. Various items belonging to Nisbet – it was of course he who lay prostrate on the carriage floor – were quickly identified. The post-mortem showed that the two bullets in his head had been fired from different guns.

With admirable promptness the Stobswood Colliery Company offered a reward of £100 for anyone providing information that would lead to the arrest of Nisbet's killer. Very quickly, Dickman became the focus of attention. The police started with an informal chat. Dickman was only too anxious to help in any way he could, or so he said. Yes, he said, he had indeed been at Newcastle Central station with Nisbet but had parted from him before the train left and had travelled in the same train but in a different compartment. Again he was apparently happy to co-operate with the police when they suggested that he should accompany them to the station and provide a signed statement. So far it was all a bit too glib.

The wheels soon started coming off the information that Dickman volunteered. Why, if he had booked to Stannington, had he somehow contrived to miss that stop and been carried on to Morpeth, the next station down the line? The incredulity of the police gathered momentum as he explained that, after paying the excess fare and leaving Morpeth station with the intention of walking back to Stannington, he had felt poorly and had rested by the side of the road. The purpose of his journey, Dickman said, was to see a man at the Dovecot Colliery. While he had been resting by the wayside, Dickman said that he had met and chatted with a man called Elliot who would vouch for him. The police took careful note of all this but decided to search his house.

Various items were removed for examination. They included some gloves which were bloodstained and some paraffin stains which might have

Alnmouth is lucky still to be on the railway network after decades which were so unkind to small wayside stations situated on main lines. Here an express of the erstwhile Great North Eastern Railway enters Alnmouth station.

suggested that attempts had been made to remove the traces of blood. No firearms were found. Dickman had something of what might be described as an 'alternative' lifestyle, spending a lot of money gambling – and usually losing. However, this was not illegal and there was nothing to suggest that the money he spent feeding his habit had been acquired dishonestly. His financial affairs were chaotic, largely it seems because he was grossly incompetent and he used a number of aliases, but again that was not actually illegal either. He admitted that a parcel containing a gun had been delivered to offices he rented in Newcastle but he claimed that it was a mistake by the company, to which he had immediately returned the gun.

All the police had were various items of largely circumstantial evidence, a suspect who they felt certain was their man and a deepening sense of frustration. The issue was how to get a case that would stand up in court. Oddly Mrs Nisbet had not at first mentioned seeing Dickman, who she knew, in the same compartment as her husband when the train had called briefly at Heaton, and she only made this revelation under closer questioning later. This was only one of a number of questions that served to confuse. However, as the days gave way to weeks it was clear that the case was going cold.

On 9 June the leather bag in which Nesbit had carried the wages was found at the bottom of a mineshaft, not far from Morpeth station and adjacent to the road along which Dickman would have walked to Stannington station. Unfortunately this bag failed to furnish any useful clues. The case went to court and Dickman was found guilty of murder. This verdict caused a storm of protest and the Home Secretary felt obliged to allow the case to be referred to the Court of Appeal.

In spite of the anomalies this court confirmed the initial verdict and the result was that Dickman was hanged at Newcastle Prison in August 1910. His last words were, 'I declare to all men I am innocent.' Forensic science was in its infancy at the time. Had modern techniques been available to them, Dickman's counsel would almost certainly have persuaded the jury to return a verdict of not guilty.

Murder at Kidsgrove

The station at Kidsgrove in North Staffordshire has experienced several changes in its name. As well as its existing name, it has also been known as Kidsgrove Junction (Harecastle), Harecastle & Kidsgrove, Harecastle and also Kidsgrove Central. This is all very confusing but in 1911 the station seems to have been named simply Harecastle. The station which was built by the North Staffordshire Railway Company still exists and is at the junction of the Crewe – Stoke and Manchester – Stoke lines, both electrified on the overhead system.

The area around Kidsgrove was formerly heavily industrialised and nearby was the very extensive Birchenwood Colliery dating back to the eighteenth century. Coking took place at the colliery complex and in 1911 an additional set of coke ovens was being constructed. It is interesting to note that the employment of foreign workers is the object of discussion in the UK in the current economic recession (2009), and that a number of German workers were employed on the contract for the building of the coke ovens. The foreman was named Lehr and among the small group of Germans was a Karl Kramer. He had been taken on because he had lived in England for some time and so he acted as an interpreter and intermediary when his fellow countrymen needed to communicate with English officialdom.

The gang of German workers were lodging in digs in Kidsgrove but Lehr, perhaps conscious of his relative status vis-à-vis his colleagues, decided to distance himself from them and take accommodation in a fine late Victorian villa not far away. He recruited Kramer and another man to help him with the removal and it is evident that during this operation Kramer had made a mental note of a cash box belonging to Lehr and the fact that it was kept in a particular drawer of a dressing table.

It seems that Kramer was something of a troublemaker because he was dismissed on 27 September 1911. He is thought to have left the area a couple of days later but was back on 2 October, being seen pedalling around the district on a bicycle. Secreted on his person were a hammer and a couple of chisels that he had surreptitiously removed from Lehr's office shortly before he had been sacked. Clearly a plan had been formulating itself in his mind.

He made his way to the villa where Lehr was staying knowing that the man would be out at work and that in the middle of the day there was a good chance that no other member of the household would be in. He broke in and made his way to Lehr's room only to be disturbed by the landlady, who was a widow, and her youngest daughter. He must have panicked for he killed them both and then also did for the housemaid who had come to see what all the commotion was about.

When the other children returned from school they were confronted with the horrible spectacle of three dead bodies. It would be hard to think of any experience more traumatic for a child but one of them at least kept their head and ran to inform authority. It was evident that robbery had been the motive of the break-in because the cash box which had contained £30 had been forced open and rifled.

Kramer left the district, complete with his trusty bicycle, and although he made efforts to alter his appearance there were several reported sightings of the fugitive over the next couple of days. On 6 October he was arrested at Doncaster, complaining bitterly that his money had been stolen by a prostitute. He was brought back to Kidsgrove by train on the same day and the tickets for the leg of the journey from Manchester, one for an adult and the other for a bicycle, are in the possession of the son of the ticket collector on duty that day.

Post-mortems on the victims showed that they had first been knocked out by Kramer and then stabbed with a chisel. Medical records produced at Kramer's trial for murder showed a history of insanity and he was adjudged unfit to plead and ordered to be detained at His Majesty's pleasure.

A Stationmaster Dies

Lintz Green was a rural wayside station in County Durham on the Derwent Valley branch line of the North Eastern Railway. In 1938 it enjoyed a roughly hourly service of trains running between Newcastle and Blackhill and, of course, vice versa. Passenger services were withdrawn in 1953. The station was fairly isolated with just a stationmaster's house and a few cottages occupied by men who worked on the track. Burnopfield, itself no metropolis, was about three miles away.

Joseph Wilson as stationmaster presided over this small outpost of the North Eastern Railway and had the proper sense of dignity and self-importance which he thought was appropriate to his rank. He was a staunch and upright man, a pillar of the Methodist community thereabouts. He may have been punctilious about company business and slightly pompous and pedantic but he had no known enemies. It was difficult to think why anybody could dislike him. Indeed it was particularly difficult to find any reason why anyone should dislike him enough to murder him. But murdered he was.

On the night of Saturday 7 October 1911 three men stood on the down platform waiting for the arrival of the last train of the day from Newcastle. They were Wilson, Fred White the booking clerk and John Routlege, the porter who was waiting for the train to take him home. The train was a few minutes late, not an uncommon happening on a Saturday night when many of the folk from the pit villages in the vicinity put on their glad rags and went off by train to sample the fleshpots of Newcastle. Their revels usually involved the consumption of copious or even excessive quantities of alcohol, and while the majority remained good-humoured incidents did sometimes occur which required the attendance of the local constabulary, causing delays.

When the train panted into the station four passengers got off. One of them was a mate of White – the booking clerk – and he waited while the latter finished his duties, which included extinguishing the few station lights that were still on. These were oil lamps which gave out a mellow, yellow glow. The other three walked down the platform ramp, crossed the line and took a field-path towards their homes in the hamlet of Low Friarside about a mile away.

Wilson saw the train off into the Stygian obscurity of the autumn night, said goodnight to White and set off for his house which was less than a hundred yards away. White's last duty of all was to lock the door to the booking office, and as he was doing so he and his friend heard a loud noise like the discharge of a firearm. They ran to the stationmaster's house just as his daughter came out hysterically shouting that her father had been shot. The shock of all this was a bit too much for White and his friend who stood as if in suspended animation trying, but unable, to decide what to do next. Help was soon at hand. The three men who had gone off to Low Friarside had also heard the shot and appeared on the scene very quickly.

One of them almost fell over Wilson's body. It was clear that the man was still alive but *in extremis* and so they carried him into the house. One of the men was experienced in what later became known as first aid but he had never seen anything as pitiful as the dying man over whom he was bending. While trying to give him some last-minute comfort and support he also wanted to elicit any information about Wilson's attacker. The stationmaster expired just as he had seemed to be summoning up his sapping energy in order to speak.

Soon a doctor and senior police officers were on the scene, not that there was much they could do until it got light. There was of course nothing they could do for poor Wilson. It appeared that he had been killed by a single bullet fired from a large calibre revolver and indeed the spent bullet was found a few yards away. A few other items were found nearby. They were unable to decide whether or not these had anything to do with the crime. The motive seemed to be robbery. Local people knew that every night Wilson carried the day's takings from the booking office the short distance to his house after the last train had left. What could not be explained for a man of such regular habits was why on this particular night he had performed this task somewhat earlier after the last train in the opposite direction had left.

A massive manhunt was launched but when it failed to produce any quick results the police found they were on the receiving end of a tidal wave of criticism orchestrated in the irresponsible and unhelpful manner often employed by the British press. However, there appeared to be a sudden breakthrough when the police decided to interview Samuel Atkinson, the relief porter at Lintz Green. He lived in Newcastle but witnesses said they had seen him hanging around the station after his shift had finished and after the time he normally caught his train home. He was arrested and charged but then it emerged that there were some procedural anomalies regarding whether or not he had been properly cautioned.

Atkinson appeared in the dock at Durham Assizes on 9 November but no sooner had the preliminaries been completed than the Chief Constable of the Durham police appeared and, to the amazement of all, told the court that no evidence was being offered against Atkinson and requesting that he be discharged. The murder was never solved and after the initial excitement Atkinson simply faded away into the obscurity which seems to have been his appointed role in life.

The railway tracks are long since gone, the formation being in use as an official footpath. Of the station there are few traces, but the platelayers' cottages and the stationmaster's house are still there, suitably modified for their role as twenty-first-century dwellings. Was Atkinson a lucky man to get away with it?

Murder at St Albans

The nominally independent Hatfield & St Albans Railway was incorporated in 1862 to build a branch line about six and a half miles long to join the two towns, the latter of which was also served by the London & North Western Railway and later by the Midland Railway. The line from Hatfield was absorbed by the Great Northern Railway who therefore gained a foothold in the territory of these two major companies with whom it did not always enjoy the most genial of relationships. Such ploys were by no means uncommon in the days of railway imperialism and sometimes led to the construction of lines which probably should never have been built.

It is unlikely that this branch line ever contributed substantially to the GNR's coffers and it led a fairly obscure existence until it closed to passengers in October 1951 and to goods and parcels traffic in 1964. The Great Northern and its successor the London & North Eastern Railway had a station located in London Road in St Albans, although trains terminated at the Abbey station where they shared facilities with the London & North Western Railway.

It was the station in London Road which provided the scenario for a brutal murder in 1918. The victim once again was the stationmaster. His name was Ellingham and in the days when the railways were a labour intensive industry he had a sizeable staff under his supervision. He was an effective and efficient manager well thought of by his staff and popular with the passengers as well as other users of the company's facilities in St Albans.

He was celebrated locally as an avid horticulturalist and he spent every moment he could in the garden attached to the stationmaster's house. His reputation as a gardener had spread beyond the confines of St Albans and he was always prepared to share his expertise with those who sought his advice. They sometimes came from considerable distances in order to pick his brains.

The downside of Mr Ellingham's life was his marriage. His wife was not a happy bunny. She never had been. Perhaps the stationmaster sometimes wondered why he had married her as he ruminated gloomily over whatever could possibly have attracted either of them to the other in the first place. Not only did she find fault with his every action, she disliked his family and was heartily disliked in return. Just about everywhere that she went she managed to antagonise all those she met. Gossip circulated, as it does, and the locals were convinced that his Trojan efforts in his garden were more the result of his desire to have some time and space away from his wife than just simply because he had 'green fingers'.

Ellingham was punctilious in those duties which are now euphemistically known as 'customer care'. This meant supervising the prompt despatch of the trains, answering questions and lending a sympathetic – but practical – ear on those rare occasions that any of the railway users had complaints. He acted as a highly effective tribune for the company in the city of St Albans and surrounding district. In fact he was so popular that when the railway company wanted to promote him to a similar role at a more important station elsewhere on their system, a petition asking them to reconsider was sent in by those in St Albans who had dealings with him.

The vox populi response these days when there has been a murder is that no one expected it to happen in a decent neighbourhood like this, or to the victim who had never made an enemy in his life. Imagine the shock and horror in St Albans when Ellingham's battered and bloodied dead body was found in the company house he occupied close to the station. He had been conspicuous by his absence from his duties on the station from early on that day, duties to which he normally paid scrupulous attention.

Staff had eventually knocked on the door of the house as his absence became a prolonged one. There was no response from within and a couple of enterprising souls had found a ladder and used it to climb up and see if he had been taken ill. Nothing could be seen. By half past eight in the evening staff had become thoroughly alarmed, and when Ellingham's daughter returned from work it was agreed that they should force entry to the house.

A horrible sight met their eyes. The stationmaster lay battered on the floor, surrounded by blood and clearly having been the victim of a violent assault. Mrs Ellingham was prostrated over a gas ring. She was still alive and it was immediately obvious that she had been deliberately breathing gas, probably in an attempt to commit suicide. This was confirmed when a suicide note of sorts was found. Letters addressed to various relations were nearby. A heavy hammer stamped with the initials 'GNR' was found bearing bloodstains. Seven wounds were found on the unfortunate Ellingham's head and it was clear that these injuries had been inflicted with the hammer. More blood-stains were found in various other parts of the house.

The authorities came to the conclusion that everyone expected, which was that Ellingham had been killed by his wife when she underwent a fit of sudden violent temper. Relations between the two of them had reached a nadir over the past period. Mrs Ellingham had become increasingly paranoid of late, being apparently resentful, even jealous, of her husband's preoccupation with his garden. She also believed that everyone down to and including the station cat were conspiring against her. It was not thought that the crime was premeditated but that it had only needed some seemingly minor provocation to turn the stationmaster's wife into a murderer. The jury found her guilty of murder and she was given a life sentence in a secure mental hospital.

The North London Railway Again

A train journey on the eve of the First World War from Chalk Farm to Broad Street station in the City of London would have offered few visual delights for anyone making the trip, had they bothered to gaze though the window at the passing scene. Were the same journey to be possible today what could be seen might have changed substantially but it would probably be every bit as dreary, although definitely not so sooty. After a slow and painful process of being run down, the pathetic remnant which was all that was left of the once fine Broad

Street station, closed in the mid-1980s. It is, however, still possible to travel on part of the route, on a train from Richmond-on-Thames to Stratford.

It is no longer possible to get on or off a train at Mildmay Park station because it closed in 1934. It was still doing business in 1914 when, on the afternoon of 8 January, a youth by the name of George Tillman climbed into an apparently empty compartment in one of the primitive, even spartan carriages operated by the North London Railway, which made up a train bound for Broad Street.

British travellers are not notably gregarious and there were always many people who chose an empty compartment whenever they could so that they could travel in solitude. Even a young man like Tillman, who was only sixteen, had already absorbed this behavioural quirk and had been gratified to find an empty compartment with ease. He could use the journey to ruminate alone and agreeably with his own thoughts. He hoped no one would intrude before his destination at Haggerston. He experienced a rapid change in mood when he realised that he was not entirely alone after all.

Under the opposite bench seat was something which looked awfully like the dead body of a small boy. Not daring to investigate, and initially rigid with terror, he tried without success to attract the attention of a railway official at Dalston. At Haggerston he left the train and managed to tell a porter abut his gory discovery. The man was too slow to prevent the train trundling off on its way but a message was telegraphed to Shoreditch, the next stop. There a member of the station staff met the train and gave the compartment a preliminary examination. The body of a curly haired little boy lay on the floor. Even to an untrained eye it was evident that the child had been strangled.

Meanwhile two women, beside themselves with worry, were desperately combing the streets of North London looking for a little boy with curly hair. The infant they were looking for was called Willie Starchfield, just five years of age; the women were his mother, Agnes, and her landlady, Emily Longstaff, from whom she rented rooms at No. 191 Hampstead Road in the Camden district.

The boy had been missing for about four hours since Emily, who had been looking after him, had sent him on an errand to a nearby shop. Agnes had been absent, engaged in a futile attempt to find employment as a seamstress. She was only too well acquainted with the pleasures but also the bitter agonies of parenthood – death had already relieved her of two children. Willie was the survivor. She had always worried about him. He was what was euphemistically known in those days as a 'delicate' child.

While the women were searching for the boy with a growing sense of apprehension, Willie's father, John Starchfield, who was estranged from Emily, would be expected to have been selling newspapers from his regular pitch at the busy junction of Oxford Street and Tottenham Court Road. There he was a well-known sight although many regarded him because of his humble role as little better than a piece of street furniture.

Indeed he did not cut a particularly impressive figure. He had once distinguished himself by bravely tackling and capturing a man who had run amok in a pub in Tottenham Court Road, receiving a bullet wound in the stomach which, a few millimetres in either direction, could easily have proved fatal at the time. This seems to have been only a short-lived aberration in his life, most of which was apparently spent attempting to avoid decisions and responsibilities. Something of a natural drifter, marriage to Agnes and parenthood could have been the making of him but after a few years of finding that the disadvantages of being a father and a husband outweighed any possible benefits, he had walked out only to end up as the denizen of a down-at-heel, louse-ridden common lodging house in Long Acre, close to Covent Garden. He had served two custodial sentences in prison for failure to provide maintenance.

The pathetic little body was readily identified as that of Willie Starchfield. Death was established as having occurred between two and three in the afternoon of the day on which the boy's corpse was discovered in the compartment of the North London Railway train. John Starchfield showed little emotion when acquainted with the fact of his son's death but he had a ready alibi. On the day of the murder, he said, he had stayed in bed at Long Acre until gone three in the afternoon, feeling the unpleasant effects of the bullet wound. This story was confirmed by another inmate of the dosshouse.

The story had been avariciously seized upon by the newspapers. They had whipped up what they chose to describe as 'public opinion' which, they said, was apparently demanding the immediate solving of the crime and the punishment of its wicked perpetrator who they had clearly already decided was Starchfield. Pieces of possible evidence came to light.

A signalman found a piece of cord by the track near Broad Street station. An eminent Home Office pathologist thought it may well have been used to strangle the child. A signalman in a signal box which the train had passed came forward to say that he had caught a glimpse of a dark-haired man apparently standing over a smaller figure with curly hair as a Chalk Farm to Broad Street train passed, just after two o'clock. These revelations provided more questions that they answered. Additional and more concrete evidence was needed. The police did not yet have enough information to make a convincing case against Starchfield.

In appearance Starchfield was dark-haired, almost Mediterranean, and his face was decorated with one of those slightly absurd droopy walrus moustaches which large numbers of men sported at the time. The police then learned that on the day in question a woman shopping in the Kentish Town Road saw a man answering Starchfield's description leading a little boy with a shock of curly hair.

This sounded like Willie and the woman had particularly noticed the couple on account of the child's hair and also the fact that he was busily engaged in devouring some kind of cake. It was a coconut cake of a sort that matched some of the contents of the luckless Willy's stomach. At the inquest she had no hesitation in picking Starchfield senior out as the man leading the child with the cake. Also at the inquest was a man who unhesitatingly pointed Starchfield out as the man he had seen with a small curly-haired boy at Camden Town station on the day which proved so fatal to little Willie.

Starchfield was charged with murder and tried at the Old Bailey but found not guilty, whereupon he was released and the newspapers then seamlessly and unblushingly converted him into the noble recipient of all that was best about the English judicial system. He died two years later of complications arising from his bullet wound.

Did Starchfield kill Willie? If he did, on a train and at the time when we can be fairly sure that the child died, how was it that no one else found the body, given that the train did at least one further return journey? He had a reputation for occasional bouts of ill-tempered violence but was he capable of cold-bloodedly killing his own child and why should he have done any such thing in the first place?

If Starchfield had got off the train after committing the murder, he must have known that it was only a matter of time before the body was discovered. Why had he not then made some attempt to hide the murder – by throwing the body out of the train, for example? How come the possible murder weapon was found near Broad Street? Had Starchfield stayed on the train to the Broad Street terminus after committing the murder and thrown it out there? And what about the alibi provided by the man who shared Starchfield's squalid sleeping quarters? Why should he lie for someone likely to face a murder charge?

Starchfield advanced his own theory that Willie had been killed for revenge purposes by friends of the man who had shot him before he made the citizen's arrest in Tottenham Court Road. Although this sounds highly fanciful the defence did produce three witnesses, two of whom attested that an hour or so before the earliest time the murder could have been committed they had seen Willie being led along the street by a woman. The third witness noted him with the woman on a bus from which they both alighted at Chalk Farm station. The tragic death of this little tousle-headed wean has never been fully explained. Nor will it ever be.

Oh What a Tangled Web We Weave...

On Wednesday 3 September 1924 Patrick Mahon was hanged at Wandsworth Prison in south-west London. He was aged only thirty-four but he had crammed an enormous amount of skulduggery and general villainy into those years. As will be explained, Mahon and his activities only tangentially concern railways, but the appalling nature of the crime for which he paid the ultimate price has never failed to attract interest.

He was an experienced embezzler and plausible con man with the looks and easy personal charm that are the stock-in-trade of his kind. Although he embezzled relatively large amounts of money, he also managed to get himself caught regularly and had to serve custodial sentences as a consequence. This suggests that he was not quite as clever as his enormous ego led him to believe.

He was a serious if not altogether successful gambler and he had a philandering habit to which he was utterly devoted, possibly to the point of obsession. He met, flattered, charmed and seduced a continuous succession of women, all of whom he abandoned totally without any scruples once they had begun to bore him and had therefore served their purpose. In spite of systematically putting it about, as it were, he was married with a wife and a home which he seemed to need in order to provide at least some kind of base or stability in his life.

His wife loyally stood by him. It appears that she had had quickly realised what kind of man she had married but seemingly accepted him for what he was and equally accepted his frequent absences 'on business', usually of a shady character. Sometimes 'on business' was a euphemism for a dirty weekend with his latest fancy woman, or for visiting the race meetings that he had repeatedly assured his wife he never attended. He was also a robber and burglar who had a violent streak. He had battered a maid with a hammer when she interrupted him while he was committing a burglary, serving time for this offence.

In 1923 Mahon established a little love nest in a bungalow on the Sussex coast between Pevensey and Eastbourne to which he brought the most recent of his conquests, a woman slightly older than himself called Emily Kaye. He was by no means averse to getting his hands on any money that his lady friends had, and he quickly found out that Emily was particularly promising in that respect because she had £400 in her bank account. She proved to be especially bad in other respects. She was a determined and forceful woman, very much in love with Mahon and intent on having him for her own. Unlike most of Mahon's women, she persisted even when it was evident that his ardour was diminishing. She simply would not take no for an answer.

She went through his things one day while he had popped out and found incriminating evidence about his illegal financial activities and at least one of his convictions. Armed with this, she made it clear that she would not be averse to a little blackmail. The police would be informed unless he agreed that they should leave the country together and live abroad. Mahon was horrified. Like most of his kind, he could hand them out but he could not take hard knocks himself. He made empty promises and played for time but nothing dented Emily's resolution. Very inconveniently, from Mahon's point of view, she also declared that she was pregnant.

It is not surprising that the couple's relationship became increasingly acrimonious. Emily found out about his embryonic relationship with a woman named Ethel and an argument developed over this and various other things. Mahon told the police that this became violent after Emily had apparently thrown an axe at him and then leapt at him, attempting to lacerate him with her fingernails. He said that he then lost his temper, hitting her and pushing her over. She fell heavily, banging her head on a coal scuttle, so he claimed, and at first he thought that she had knocked herself out. Shortly afterwards to his horror he realised that she was dead, so he said. It was, Mahon glibly assured the officers, an accident. The date almost certainly was 14 April.

Mahon had not allowed the problems he was embroiled in with Emily to get too much in the way of his continuing shenanigans with other women. On several occasions he had left Emily at the bungalow and gone up to London 'on business'. On one such occasion, on 10 April, he had met a young lady by the name of Ethel Duncan for the first time. By dint of using every drop of charm he possessed he managed to get her to agree to a date. He would call her up soon, he said, when he had attended to various bits of business. He did not enlarge on what these involved. This is hardly surprising because one of these 'bits of business' involved a visit to a hardware shop in London SW1 where he purchased a large butcher's knife and a meat saw, probably on 12 April.

On 15 April Mahon telegraphed Ethel asking her to meet him at Charing Cross the next day. The story becomes almost surreal at this point. Mahon turned up with his wrist bandaged, telling her that he had received this injury when he had fallen off a bus. He had of course sustained it during his scrap with Emily. Ethel and Mahon had a candlelit dinner during which he wooed her for all he was worth, and the successful outcome of all his efforts was a promise that she would spend a weekend away with him.

Ethel duly arrived at Eastbourne on 18 April and was elated and flattered to receive such a rapturous welcome from Mahon who, after all, was really little more than a stranger. The couple spent the following three days and nights largely engaged in energetic and no doubt passionate bouts of love-making. Ethel's participation in this activity might have been rather less that fervid had she known that a few feet away in a trunk in a room which Mahon kept locked lay the dismembered remains of her paramour's previous sexual partner. The butcher's knife and meat saw had already played their appointed role in this unfolding drama.

On Monday 21 April Ethel and Mahon travelled up to London, he ostensibly being engaged 'on business'. The next day he returned to the bungalow and set about disposing of Emily's physical remains. He then gratefully made his way home. His wife welcomed him back from his 'business trip' knowing full well that it had almost certainly involved some heavy-duty philandering. This time, however, she found that he was behaving very strangely.

Normally he acted with total sang-froid and happily lied through his teeth if quizzed about his activities. Jessie, his wife, had largely learned not to probe too deeply but she quickly realised that this time there was something different about her husband. He seemed jittery and snappy. Such behaviour was of course not surprising given that he had just branched out to include murder in his bulging portfolio of multifarious criminal activities.

This is where the railway connection comes in. Normally sanguine about her husband's quirks and peccadilloes, Jessie now felt that there was something amiss and she took the opportunity while he was out to go through his things. This was not the kind of thing she would normally do and was a measure of the unease she felt. She found a cloakroom ticket issued at Waterloo station. She mentioned her suspicions to a friend who happened to be a retired police officer and he surrendered the ticket at the cloakroom receiving in exchange a canvas bag. This was opened to reveal a knife and bloodstained female clothing. Our ex-police friend then acted with great canniness. He deposited the bag back into storage and informed the police, who agreed to watch and wait for Mahon to turn up to retrieve it. Understandably, they thought that he might be able to help them to elucidate a few points about which they were curious.

The surveillance was slow in bringing results but it was eureka at half past six on the evening of 2 May. Mahon turned up to reclaim the bag, was instantly arrested and then blurted out the first thing which came into his head. This was that he could account for any bloodstains which had been found in the bag – he had used it for carrying dog's meat. He was less fulsome when he was informed that tests showed that the traces of blood in the bag were human. Also which dog was this that he was so generously feeding? He did not have a dog. He did not even like them. Swiftly recovering his composure, however, he told his interrogators that he would now come clean. He had butchered her body, he said, because no one would believe his story about how Emily had died and he was afraid that he himself might even have come under suspicion of having murdered her! A response to this might be 'perish the thought'.

Ongoing investigations could not find any evidence in the doorframe that an axe had been forcefully thrown at him only to miss him and go on to hit the woodwork. Reassembling Emily's bodily parts was a painstaking task for the pathologists and left uncompleted because her head was never found, but on the evidence available it was thought that Mahon had either strangled her or battered her with the axe. The jury had little difficulty in deciding that he was guilty of the murder.

The main entrance to Waterloo station. The Victory Arch was opened in 1922 as a War Memorial for employees of the London & South Western Railway who died in the First World War.

Mahon was a seasoned railway traveller, using trains to take him both to genuine business meetings – including those with crooked dealings in mind – and to his various amorous trysts. The canvas bag recovered from the Waterloo cloakroom he had taken with him on a train from Eastbourne to London with various items of Emily's anatomy wrapped up in brown paper. He had intended to throw these from the carriage windows at various points along the line but he found to his chagrin that the train was too crowded to allow him to do this. He had to dispose of them randomly elsewhere, and it was the unpredictable placing of these gory relics that gave the pathologists so many headaches in trying to reconstruct the body of the unfortunate Emily Kaye.

Mahon showed many of the classic symptoms of psychopathy. He was amoral and ruthless, he made a career out of dishonesty and duplicity, he appeared to lack any sense of remorse and was seemingly totally indifferent to the judicial process and the sense of what is socially right and wrong, which the criminal law and the penal system, no matter how imperfectly, attempts to implement.

The Girl who Never got to the Station

In August 1881, the London, Brighton & South Coast Railway Co. opened a line from Eridge to Polegate, giving access from the Tunbridge Wells area to the Sussex coast at Eastbourne. This route became known affectionately as the 'Cuckoo Line', which gives some sense of the delightful rural scenery through which it passed.

In 1926 Emma Alice Smith, aged sixteen, set off on her bicycle from the village of Waldron to her local railway station nearby. This station had a number of name changes over the years but it was generally known as 'Waldron and Horam'. Unfortunately Emma never got there. Her death remains an unsolved murder.

In 2008 a descendent of Emma's family told the police that back in 1953 a dying man had confessed to Emma's sister that he was responsible for her murder. He claimed to have killed her and then thrown her weighted body into a pond and disposed of the bicycle. When this revelation was made the family decided that it was best to keep quiet, and so it was more than fifty years later that the embargo on the information was lifted. It is unlikely that the details of the murder will ever come to light. Perhaps this is no bad thing.

The latest news in February 2009 is that the police are going to reopen the case.

The Left Luggage Horror

The railways no longer handle parcels and small consignments but they do, somewhat unwillingly, place lockers for left luggage in a number of major stations and there are still a few stations which operate a left luggage office. These are convenient for those wanting to leave a few items of hand luggage while they perhaps go and explore the town. Back in 1927 a new shade of meaning was added to the word 'deposit'. Someone 'deposited' a large black trunk at the left luggage office at London's Charing Cross station of the Southern Railway. 'Deposited' in the trunk was the dismembered body of a woman.

There was nothing particularly unusual about such large items as trunks being left in the temporary care of the railway and it is unlikely that the station worker who accepted payment for it and found it a shelf would have turned a hair. It would have been all in a day's work. Anyway, the reasons why

Waldron & Horeham Road station. A Standard 2-6-4T heads a local train at the station which had changed little since the days of the London, Brighton & South Coast Railway.

someone should wish such a trunk to be stored were the depositor's business, and likewise the nature of its contents. The contents ceased to be a private matter, however, when the trunk started to exude an appalling stench.

It was opened and it was evident that not only were there human remains inside but they were the remains of someone who had died some while previously. The body parts were in brown paper parcels, but a leading pathologist was able to state that death had been due to asphyxia as the result of strangling and that the woman had been dead for at least a week. The initials 'I.F.A' were on the lid of the trunk and a label bore the name 'F. Austin, St Leonards'. There was some blood-stained clothing. One item bore the name 'P. Holt'. Others had what appeared to be laundry marks, including '447' and what looked something like '588'.

There was a rush to get around to the home of F. Austin at St Leonards but the police were quickly satisfied that he had nothing to do with the trunk. It was extremely unfortunate that the paperwork relating to the depositing of the trunk was missing. The police thought that this was carelessness and that there were no sinister connotations. Doubtless the railway worker involved got a rollicking.

Enquiries were made about the shops that sold such trunks, either new or second-hand, and photographs of the trunk, its contents and an appeal for help were published in the press. The line of enquiry concerning the shops proved to be of little help, but someone called Holt living in Chelsea got in touch with the police as a result of seeing the appeal in the paper. One of the blood-stained items in the trunk, the police were told, belonged to a Miss P. Holt. The body in the trunk, however, was not a deceased member of the Holt family but that of a female cook who had worked for them briefly. The Holts did not know what had happened to the woman concerned, whose name was Roles, but they believed that she had been married.

In fact the woman in the trunk did indeed call herself Roles but she had lived with, rather than been married to, the Mr Roles who the police traced quickly. His story was that they had cohabited for some years but the relationship had cooled, and after a fair amount of bickering she had left. On the face of it this story gave Mr Roles a motive for murder, but after further enquiries the police were convinced that he was not the killer and so they concentrated on trying to find out more about the dead woman, her movements and her associates.

She turned out to be a prostitute named Minnie Bonati and she was married to an Italian waiter from whom she had long been estranged. He in turn was interviewed but was also able to satisfy the police that he was not involved. A general dealer in second-hand goods with a shop in downtown Brixton then volunteered the information that he had sold the – by now nationally famous – trunk to a man whose appearance he was unfortunately unable to recall.

Police investigations involve much unglamorous but painstaking and meticulous information gathering and the pursuit of trails which often turn out to be dead ends. On occasions sheer happenstance helps the police with their enquiries. In this case an entirely new, and what turned out to be extremely fruitful, line of enquiry was embarked upon – all by the merest of chances.

Older readers may remember shoeblacks who, mostly in busy parts of central London, provided a boot and shoe polishing service, for a fee of course. Although some of them had well-established pitches and a regular and appreciative clientele it always seemed to be a hard way to make a living. Anyway, a shoeblack just happened to pick up a small crumpled piece of paper which when unravelled proved to be a ticket giving details of the deposit of a large trunk at Charing Cross station.

Like everyone else he had heard about the body in the trunk, and, thinking that this ticket might provide vital clues, he went to the police. They pounced on it with glee because it gave the date that the trunk was deposited – 6 May.

Now they had the date and soon they had the time, having traced the person who had the preceding ticket. It was a woman who had arrived at the station by taxi.

It was obvious that whoever had deposited the trunk could not have carried it to Charing Cross so they turned their attention to the cabbies and porters at the station. They found a cabbie who distinctly remembered a fare he had taken from Westminster to the station on the day in question. He was accompanied by an unusually large black trunk which could only just be fitted in the back of the cab. Not only was it unusually large, it was also unwontedly heavy. He had helped the man to get the trunk in the back of the taxi and had commented about its weight. 'It contains books,' the man had quickly replied.

Soon after these revelations another plum landed unexpectedly in the lap of the police. A bus conductor came forward who remembered helping a man on board his bus with an extremely large and heavy trunk. The conductor was sure the date was 6 May. The conductor had been extremely unhappy about taking the trunk because it obstructed the rear platform, but he was a kind-hearted Cockney used to life's rough-and-tumble and he liked to help people out whenever he could. The man had booked to Victoria but had alighted instead at Rochester Row in Westminster, a couple of stops short. It had been just as much of a palaver to get the blinking trunk off the bus.

The investigations were becoming more convoluted by the hour, although the police were convinced that they were on the right trail. The cabbie had picked up the fare and the trunk in Rochester Row close to a block of offices at No. 86. There was little residential property in the area and it therefore seemed a reasonable bet that whoever the mystery fare was, he probably had some connection with this or another block of offices nearby. The police decided to question everyone who worked in the vicinity and started with the nearest block. They struck gold immediately.

Many of those who worked in this particular building remembered a very large black trunk which, because it was there for a few days, was creating an increasingly irritating obstruction in a corridor. It was rumoured that the trunk contained ledgers and other items relating to one of several companies that had occupied offices in the building but had gone bust. This was, after all, the economic depression of the inter-war years.

Ongoing enquiries established that a firm run by a John Robinson had hired a suite of offices a few months previously but had apparently gone bust and vacated them. A cheque he had paid for the rent was traced to the landlord and Robinson's address obtained. This was in Camberwell but he had moved away – significantly on 6 May – announcing to all and sundry that he was moving to Lancashire. It was subsequently found that he had actually moved to the Kennington district of south London, not far from Camberwell.

The gaunt prison on the Pentonville Road was completed in 1842. It retains its baleful presence to this day.

Everyone was now on the lookout for Mr John Robinson. On 19 May he was seen near Elephant and Castle and was accosted by the police who asked him ever so politely if he would be so good as to come with them to the station and help to elucidate a few matters they were looking into. He assured them that he was only too happy to help in any way he could and he provided full, and seemingly very plausible, answers – or were they somehow too glib?

Robinson had been a real rolling stone, turning his hand to all manner of jobs, seemingly legal at first but branching out into illegality when he married bigamously. Still, that peccadillo was not germane to the current investigation, and the police continued to listen closely to a long and rambling discourse of his comings and goings on the days leading up to 6 May. He coolly denied knowing anything about a Minnie Bonati. Robinson was affable, even charming, but there was something about him that did not quite ring true.

It was decided to put him in an identity parade to see whether the man who had sold him the trunk and the taxi driver who took Robinson and the

The chapel at Pentonville Prison. Here prisoners kept under the 'Silent System' were harangued on the hellfire waiting for them if they did not redeem their sins.

trunk to Charing Cross could pick him out – they did not. Reluctantly the police let him go but then turned their attention to a minute examination of the office he had occupied in Rochester Row. A few items were found which had some traces of blood on them, and a towel with a sewn-in name which was traced to a pub in which he had worked behind the bar.

They still did not have any irrefutable evidence but they decided to have Robinson in again for questioning and to rough him up a bit psychologically. If he was guilty of Minnie's murder then he was certainly a cool character. However, they went at it hard and it seems that the tension was getting to him and he began to crack up. With little prompting he made a full confession.

He had met Minnie at Victoria station – perhaps we could say that he picked her up there. Presumably they had sex in mind and they went back to his office where he finished a number of letters while she waited, apparently with increasing impatience. It was hardly flattering for her ego as he sat there banging away on a typewriter doing essential correspondence. Eventually she told him that she needed some money. Robinson told the police that when he refused to give her any she became abusive and started to swear at him.

He suddenly decided he had had enough, and to silence the foul-mouthed harridan he picked up a poker and hit her on the head whereupon she fell against the fireplace banging her head again. He said he then went home but when he returned the next day, he found that she was dead. He was dumbfounded and confused, he said, and in a panic he bought a knife and cut Minnie's body up, placing the pieces in the trunk and disposing of the knife by burying it on Clapham Common. He then called a cab and, accompanied by the trunk, made for Charing Cross where the trunk was placed in left luggage.

There were a few questionable points in all this but the police were certain they had got their man and he duly appeared in court charged with murder. In court it was demonstrated that Minnie's injuries were such as could not have been caused by falling on a hard object. Certainly she had been hit, probably knocked unconscious, and then strangled. The trial took place at the Old Bailey and the execution was at Pentonville on 12 August 1927.

You Need Trunks When You go to Brighton in Sussex-by-the-Sea

Nowhere else in Britain is quite like Brighton. It has always managed to exude a unique combination of elegance and raffishness. In reality parts of it have always been downright tawdry or worse. It has rejoiced in any number of nicknames, some affectionate, others opprobrious, over the last four centuries. Probably no other place in Britain with the exception of London, Edinburgh and Bath has been more written and talked about.

W.M. Thackeray (1811–63), the novelist, described it in 1848 as, 'Brighton that always looks brisk, gay and gaudy, like a harlequin's jacket.' Now in the twenty-first century it is probably associated in the popular mind with party conferences, a nudist beach, the gaunt remains of a once splendid pleasure pier, dirty weekends, magnificent Regency architecture, day trips from London, the gay scene, foreign language students, the London to Brighton Vintage Car Run and possibly Richard Attenborough's extremely unconvincing perform-ance as a rookie gangster called 'Pinkie' in the film *Brighton Rock* made in 1947 and based on the novel of the same name written by Graham Greene.

Brighton is not a resort made by the railways in the sense that such a description can be applied to Blackpool, Skegness or Cleethorpes, for exam-ple. Brighton had already established itself as a favoured and fashionable seaside watering place in the eighteenth century long before the first railway to the town was opened in 1841. This was the line from London and its arrival changed the character of Brighton, allowing it to offer itself as the place for a day trip for lower-middle class and better-paid working class people from London. It also became a dormitory for substantial numbers of workers in well-paid employment who could now live by the sea and work in London, these being commuters before the word had been invented.

The changing, more demotic character of Brighton was reflected in the fact that Queen Victoria stayed there for the last time in 1845. Clearly she had no desire to get too close to her subjects, particularly the more proletarian ones. The social and other ramifications of the changes brought by the railway are beyond the remit of this book, but suffice it to say that the railway has always had a significant presence in what, since 2000, has become the City of Brighton and Hove.

It still has a large central station with a magnificent overall roof and the London Road viaduct which towers above and absolutely dominates the quarter of the city over which it passes. It formerly had the locomotive and rolling stock workshops of the London, Brighton & South Coast Railway, and unusually for such an important town and key railway centre it was only ever served by one main line railway company.

Sunday 17 June 1934 was an almost oppressively hot day and Brighton station was doing a roaring trade with day trippers from the metropolis coming to sample its delights and perhaps have a dip in the cooling sea. Brighton was, after all, 'Old Ocean's Bauble'. By contrast with the bustle around the concourse and platforms, the left luggage office was almost somnolent, few people having a use for its services on such a day. It was also stuffy and, as the day wore on, increasingly smelly.

It was not difficult to locate the source of what could only be described as a stench. It was enough to make the two men working in the office retch – and it did. It was a plywood, canvas-covered and clearly very new trunk which had been deposited on the floor because of the weight of whatever it contained precluded it from being placed on the shelves. What on earth could it contain that was producing such an appallingly offensive odour?

The men had their suspicions that the smell was organic with a markedly sinister putrid tinge to it, and they must have remembered the sensational story of the body in the trunk at Charing Cross station in 1927; it had, after all, only been seven years previously. They decided that they had had enough and they spoke to a railway police officer about it. Accompanied by an officer from the county constabulary, this man confirmed the source of the smell and concluded, not without misgivings such was the gagging stink that assailed his nostrils, that the trunk and its contents should be opened and investigated. This was indeed a daunting prospect and it must have been with some sense of relief that both officers quickly agreed that they needed to refer the situation to higher authority.

The outcome of this initiative was the swift arrival on the scene of a Detective Constable. He knew what had to be done but it was another matter actually doing it. Summoning every ounce of fortitude he possessed he prised the trunk open whereupon the smell became even worse. He had to rush out onto the concourse several times and gratefully inhale the smell of the station, which by comparison was like the scent of freshly mown meadows. In between he investigated the contents of the trunk.

He was soon joined by another plain clothes officer and the three of them probed something emitting the foulest smell imaginable and, perhaps fortunately, wrapped in brown paper. The police officers did not need to be geniuses to know even before it was opened that the parcel contained mortal remains, probably human and in an advanced stage of putrescence. A female human torso was soon transfixing their horrified eyes.

Within minutes the area was cordoned off and the local constabulary top brass had arrived on the scene. The trunk, complete with its gruesome contents, was removed to the mortuary. All the other items deposited in the left luggage facility were scrutinised to see if the other bodily parts could be located, but without success. However, by extraordinary coincidence, other human remains were found. They were those of a baby girl who had clearly died within days of being born and had presumably been placed there by her mother, perhaps to hide the stigma of illegitimacy. These remains had been there for about five months and the officers quickly ruled out any connection with the current investigation.

There were a number of items in the trunk along with the torso but they did little more than add to the questions that the police wanted answering. Who was the woman in the trunk whose remains showed that she had been so brutally butchered? Left luggage facilities on both railway and bus stations throughout southern England were scoured. An appeal went out for anyone to contact the police if a female relative or friend had gone missing. Surely somebody would come forward, surely some clues would turn up.

News came from King's Cross station in London where a search of the left luggage depository had located a scruffy suitcase emitting an increasingly revolting smell. Inside, wrapped in brown paper soaked in blood and what was apparently olive oil, were two legs and two feet. It did not take the experts long to establish without any doubt that these items were the missing legs and feet. It was a mighty step forward but who was the mystery woman to whom these bits and pieces belonged?

The leading Home Office pathologist Sir Bernard Spilsbury established that the victim of what had been an appalling murder had been a healthy middle-class woman aged between twenty-one and twenty-eight. She had been pregnant. The case had been placed in the left luggage facility on 7 June, which was the day after the stinking trunk had been left at Brighton station.

It is a known fact in the natural world that lightning can strike twice or more in the same place. The finding of human remains in trunks in the same town within a few weeks of each other is less common. We now switch to a seedy little chancer, a Londoner who posed as being an Italian – which he was not – but who managed to make a decent fist of looking the part. He thought it made him more exotic and attractive to women. He went by a number of aliases, one of which we will use which was 'Tony Mancini'.

He was in and out of casual employment and filled in-between times with petty crime and small-scale swindles. In June 1934 he was working as a general factotum in a café overlooking Brighton beach. He had something of an on-off relationship with a woman whose name was Violet but who wished to be known as 'Violette' – again this was thought to sound vaguely foreign and exotic. The couple cohabited despite the fact that she was actually still married and they shared a succession of down-at-heel flats and bedsitters, first in downmarket districts of London and then in similar parts of Brighton.

She resented her failed attempt to make a career as a dancer and she also resented the fact that she was getting older and losing whatever looks she had had. Jobs were hard to come by and so she operated, sporadically and a little half-heartedly, as a prostitute with Mancini constituting himself her pimp. They both felt that life had dealt them a lousy set of cards and were resentful and disillusioned. They were bored and irritated with each other and had frequent rows.

Their growing mutual antipathy culminated on the evening of 10 May 1934 with a violent row and with Mancini hurling a coal-hammer at the lady in his life. It is probable that he had not really intended to hit her at all, but on this occasion he threw the missile with all the accuracy of a Bisley marksman. When he realised that he had killed Violet, he did not know what to do. He left her where she lay for a few hours but then, realising that her body needed to be put somewhere out of sight, he managed with difficulty to manoeuvre it in an upright position into a wardrobe, a task made difficult by the onset of rigor mortis.

After a few days he decided to move to another flat, in this case close to the railway station, and he placed Violet's body in a trunk he bought specially for the purpose. He recruited two acquaintances to help him move the trunk onto a barrow and across town to the new address. Once moved into his new quarters, and with a suitable cover bought specially for the purpose, Mancini used the trunk as a place for any visitors to sit on. One or two visitors did come round and commented on an unpleasant smell around the flat. This smell was difficult to identify and it was difficult to pinpoint exactly where it was coming from. None of the few guests realised that they were sitting on a trunk which contained the source of the increasingly nauseating aroma.

The reader must wonder about Mancini's mindset as he continued to go to work only to return nightly to a flat containing a trunk from which the rotting body fluids of his former mistress were oozing and permeating the whole place with an increasingly foul stench. Mancini had little interest in the news or current affairs and it therefore came as a shock when he saw a local newspaper with a headline about a body in a trunk being found in the town. His heart must have been in his mouth until he ascertained that this gory find had been made at the railway station. He relaxed – no one else knew about Violet's death and the whereabouts of her torso or other remains.

A massive murder hunt was launched bringing in the services of Scotland Yard. Major lines of enquiry included following up all the reports of missing women and all women who had been receiving pre-natal advice and treatment. The police spread their net across the whole country on these enquiries. Door-to-door enquiries were carried out in Brighton and surrounding areas. Police had to deal with dozens of reports of sinister-looking men humping equally sinister-looking packages around or pushing them on carts or handbarrows. Most of these turned out to be easily explained and entirely innocent although they took time to be checked out which of course they had to be.

There was the usual crop of hoaxes and honest, well-intentioned but time-wasting misunderstandings. An appeal to those who had been at Brighton station on the day the trunk had been deposited produced many responses but the only useful one was that it seemed highly likely that the trunk had been brought to Brighton on a train, and almost certainly from one of the stations not far away on the coast line and certainly not beyond Worthing. With a collective sigh the police decided to re-interview all those who had already been quizzed for information and to use different detectives. This was a long, tedious and drawn-out process, but if the dead woman was local, surely someone must have noticed her unexplained absence.

The dingy house in which Mancini had his flat and to which he had moved the trunk containing Violet's body was badly in need of re-pointing and a firm had been taken on to do the job. Scaffolding went up around the building but it was not long before the workmen were complaining about the horrible smell that was emanating from somewhere low down in the building. Indeed so bad was the smell that the foreman decided to notify the police. Officers were detailed to investigate and had to agree that the smell was that of rotting flesh.

The owners of the house were away, and as no one else responded to the repeated knockings they decided to force the front door open. They gained access to Mancini's quarters and homed in on a trunk which seemed to be the source of the smell. Retching almost uncontrollably the officers prised the trunk open and inside of course was the body of a woman. She was in an advanced stage of decomposition and myriads of large, prosperous-looking grubs were gorging themselves happily on her remains. Brighton now had a second trunk murder!

Sir Bernard Spilsbury found himself making a return visit to Brighton. He showed that the woman had been killed by a violent blow with a heavy blunt instrument. Enquiries quickly elicited who she was and her relationship with Mancini, who, feeling a growing sense of unease, had already decamped for London where he hoped to achieve anonymity until things quietened down. A description of Mancini was circulated throughout the UK. The description included mention of the rather odd way in which he walked.

On the evening of 18 July two police officers were sitting, rather bored, in their patrol car close to a pub in Lewisham, south-east London, when they saw a man walk past heading for an all-night café. There was something so distinctive about the way in which he walked that they immediately recalled the circular they had read about a man wanted for questioning concerning the finding of a dead woman in a trunk in Brighton.

They arrested the man, who readily admitted that his name was Mancini, and overnight he found himself being whisked at high speed down the A23 to Brighton. He appeared at the magistrates' court the next morning. He was remanded in custody on a charge of murder. Soon he found himself the star turn at a murder trial at Lewes Assizes. This is a role that brought out the hitherto unsuspected thespian in him. He lied through his teeth and quite unashamedly and histrionically tried to play the jury.

He had returned one night to the flat that he shared with Violet only to find her dead, he said. He had not reported the death because he claimed that a man like himself with a record of various petty criminal offences would never be treated fairly by the police. Yes he knew it had been stupid but he had decided to move Violet's body in a trunk to another flat. All this, you understand, between gulps, sobs, snuffles, tears coursing down his face and silences while he tried to cope with the emotional trauma he was undergoing. It may not have won an Oscar but it did win a verdict of 'not guilty'. Mancini walked away from the court a free man.

What about the dead baby? The enquiries continued; they went nowhere. The senior officer in charge of the enquiry accumulated pieces of evidence to suggest that the woman – Violet – might have visited a member of the medical profession to obtain an abortion. The performance of an abortion was illegal. Perhaps the abortion went wrong and Violet died. The father of the unborn child and the back-street abortionist would have been anxious to keep what had happened secret. Perhaps they therefore dismembered Violet's body and placed it in the trunk which was then deposited in the left luggage facility at Brighton station.

A possible performer of the abortion was identified and upon being questioned smiled unctuously and issued a veiled threat that he had friends in very high places who would not only ensure his immunity from prosecution but would be able to make things very difficult for any overzealous police officers who attempted to proceed with their enquiries. The murderer of Violet was never brought to justice.

Murder in the South Side

Pollokshields East is a station serving the Cathcart Circle line on the edge of Glasgow's smart South Side late nineteenth and early twentieth-century suburbs. The Cathcart Circle was immortalised in a characterful novel by

R.W. Campbell called *Snooker Tam of the Cathcart Railway*, published in 1919. The eponymous Tam is a lively and cheeky young station lad at the fictional Kirkbride station on the line, who gets into various scrapes with his elders and betters and finds many sonsie lasses to flirt with while he attends – or does not attend – to his platform duties.

Snooker Tam may be a cheerful and light-hearted read but there was nothing light-hearted about events at Pollokshields East around half past seven on the evening of 10 December 1945. It was a freezing night and three railway workers were sitting round the fire in the stationmaster's office, glad of the respite from the cutting winds outside. They were Kerith Scott, an experienced railway employee who could turn his hand to just about any task around a railway station, a young junior porter called Robert Brown and a female clerk called Joan Bradshaw.

The three were chatting in a desultory fashion when suddenly a door burst open and a man opened fire with a revolver, aiming cold-bloodedly at each of them in turn. The woman was hit and she died immediately while Brown received injuries from which he died the next day. Scott was the lucky one. He was only grazed by the bullet fired at him. The intruder escaped clutching two metal boxes which he clearly hoped contained the day's takings. They were actually empty.

A massive investigation was immediately set in motion by the police. The dying Brown managed to provide some kind of description, including the fact that the murderer seemed to be wearing 'de-mob' clothes. The net was thrown far and wide. Large numbers of people who had been in the vicinity of Pollokshields East about that time were traced and quizzed but with little result, and after six months the police had to admit that they were no further forward. It was therefore almost in desperation that a reward of £1,000 was offered to anyone providing information that led to the arrest and conviction of the murderer. Various cranks and time-wasters came forward but no useful information was gained. What could the police do that they had not already done?

On the morning of 9 October 1946, ten months after the murder at Pollokshields East, a police constable was on duty not far from Cathcart railway station on the same line when a young man walked up to him and requested that the officer accompany him to the police station because he wanted to confess to a murder. Was the man who made this revelation just another time-waster? The constable did not particularly want a rollicking from his sergeant for inviting a nutter into the police station but he would get an even bigger rocket if it turned out later that the man was indeed a murderer and he, the officer, had told him to go away.

He decided to play cautiously and to ask the man a few questions. The answers he gave made it clear that he was claiming to be the killer in the Pollokshields East murder. He had been living with the horror of what he had

Pollokshields East station on the Cathcart Circle Line in Glasgow's southern inner suburbs. A recent picture, showing the unprepossessing building which replaced an attractive Caledonian Railway installation with a fine umbrella canopy.

done for all those months, he said, and had tried to commit suicide by shooting himself but his gun had jammed. Concluding that the fates were against him, he therefore decided to turn himself in.

The investigating officers were understandably a little sceptical about his story, but when Kerith Scott picked him out in an identity parade as the man who had shot him at Pollokshields East on that dreadful night the previous December, they knew they had their man. He was a railway fireman and they charged him with the murder of Joan Bradshaw and Robert Brown and a number of other offences connected with the murder.

Immediately the issue of insanity was raised. The young man was examined by a panel of experts who concluded that while he was definitely mentally abnormal, he was not certifiably insane and had known the difference between right and wrong when he had committed the murder. The issue of insanity went on to be at the centre of the subsequent trial but a majority of the jury did not accept the plea of diminished responsibility and found him guilty. He was sentenced to death but reprieved on appeal, receiving a life sentence instead. Was he a young man living in a fantasy world of gun-toting or was he a cold-blooded killer prepared to murder entirely without conscience in the pursuit of robbery?

An Inhumane Killer

On a February day in 1936 Mr Arthur Mead took an early evening train at Aylesbury heading up to London, though his destination was High Wycombe. A Mrs Fuller joined the train at Princes Risborough and sat in an adjacent compartment. Just as the train was heading southwards through the tunnel near Saunderton on the Great Western & Great Central line she heard a sharp report followed by another shortly afterwards. She could not say exactly what the sound reminded her of but it made her uneasy.

She stuck her head out of the carriage window but there was nothing to be seen. When she arrived at her destination, High Wycombe, she alighted and noticed a man slumped on the seat in the compartment next to the one she had been travelling in. Perhaps he was asleep because he certainly looked dead to the world. Miss Fuller continued on her way, thinking nothing more about it.

The train changed guards at High Wycombe and the man who was taking over, Wood by name, walked the length of the train peering into each compartment to get an idea of the number of passengers and to ensure that all was as it should be. He spotted a man who was slumped in a compartment and looking distinctly unwell. He alerted one of the station clerks. The train left High Wycombe but when it arrived at Beaconsfield, Wood decided to take another look at his woebegone passenger. His condition was clearly deteriorating and Wood decided that he needed to be taken off the train.

He enlisted the help of a porter. Bingham, for that was the porter's name, knew first aid and did what he could for the man who seemed weak and confused but who then suddenly blurted out that he had been shot by a stranger toting a revolver. A doctor soon arrived and confirmed that he had indeed been shot in the chest and that he was in such a bad way that he would not last long.

Two police sergeants arrived at the station and had to try to extract as much information as they could decently do before the victim of the shooting expired. They established that he was Arthur Mead from High Wycombe and he had got on the train at Aylesbury. He told them that at Princes Risborough a man who he did not know had entered his compartment and shot him with a revolver. He provided a description of a man in his mid-twenties and details of his appearance. Mead provided all this information with almost his last dying breath and his life was extinguished shortly afterwards.

The compartment of the carriage in which Mead had travelled was subjected to minute scrutiny by the police. There was no sign of struggle but a spent bullet was found in the kind of position consistent with the victim being shot from the front while being in a seated position. Mead's overcoat provided evidence that the muzzle of a gun had been placed against it and fired from that position. Where was this weapon? If it could be found, it might elucidate some of the unanswered questions.

They did not have to wait for long but they were mightily surprised when it turned up. A track worker found a gun lying by the side of the line along which Mead's train had travelled. Like a good citizen he handed it in and the police were, to use that ugly but descriptive modern word, gobsmacked. It was a humane killer of the sort used to despatch animals in an abattoir. It had not been very humane in this instance because it had fired the bullet that fatally injured Mead. What kind of a murderer used such a weapon? Was this the first time in history that a humane killer had possibly been used for the purposes of murder?

Question now piled on top of question. Miss Fuller said that she had distinctly heard two reports. If the gun had been fired twice, where was the second bullet? If it had actually only been fired once what, if anything, was it that she heard the second time? How come there was no trace of Mead's supposed killer? What kind of a killer would apparently just pick a victim in such a random fashion or did Mead have an enemy? Did Mead actually kill himself? If so it stretched the bounds of credibility to suppose that he had held the gun against himself, fired it sustaining his appalling injury, got up onto his feet, lowered the compartment window and thrown the gun out.

Additionally the gun was found further down the line than Saunderton, which was just to the south of Princes Risborough. Even more incredible was the notion that he had shot himself and received the fatal injury, sat in agony for some minutes and then, almost as an afterthought, had thrown the gun out of the train. If he had fired the gun himself in the act of committing suicide, why lie about the stranger who shot him? Those people who are aware that they are dying do not usually lie when uttering their valedictory words. If Mead had killed himself, what was the reason?

Mead was a butcher by trade but had been working in a knacker's yard. He had fought in the army during the First World War and, although physically uninjured, he had been mentally scarred and was unable to get over the sights and sounds he had experienced. He had severe mental health problems and his doctor had only recently recommended that he should undertake treatment as in-patient in an appropriate hospital.

He had owned two humane killers and although he had got rid of the more modern of the two, which was of the captive bolt type, he had kept the old-fashioned bullet one. His wife felt almost certain that the gun retrieved by the police was of this sort. As the police pursued their enquiries they found that Mead had been trying to borrow some money. What for?

An inquest was held which concluded that Mr Arthur Mead took his own life when he was not of sound mind. At the time many people felt that this was a not an appropriate verdict because it left so many questions unanswered. No further evidence has come to light that could be used to answer those questions.

Murder on the Aberdeen Express?

Britain was still in a state of post-war austerity in 1950. The London & North Eastern Railway had been in dire financial straits before the Second World War, despite the glamorous image of the streamlined expresses reaching speeds of 100mph and more on the East Coast Main Line. The demands of the war had just about brought it and the other three companies of the 'Big Four' to their knees, and nationalization just after the war had been necessary to prevent them collapsing completely.

Great efforts were being made to improve things although there were still many disgruntled passengers. Not so the young Women's Royal Air Force Corporal stationed at RAF Leuchars who was standing on the down platform at Leuchars Junction waiting for an afternoon train to Aberdeen. With her was the young man, also in the RAF, who was 'dating' her. She was a widow and he was married but estranged from his wife who refused to divorce him. Both of them were travelling northwards to spend Christmas with their respective families in Aberdeen. Their relationship was not an easy one despite the various interests they shared. They had frequent rows.

They joined the already crowded train and had no option but to stand in the corridor where they proceeded to have an audible row, embarrassing for nearby passengers. Soon after the train left Arbroath a passenger complained to the guard that the toilet had been occupied for what seemed like half an hour or more. The guard knocked on the door to be answered by a man's voice. He opened the door, coming out looking somewhat bothered and confused. The guard could also see a woman in the tiny compartment but it was quickly established that she was dead. The man was arrested and charged with murder which was quickly changed to 'culpable homicide'.

Medical examination of the woman demonstrated that she had a heart condition which made her especially vulnerable to the effects of shock. It seems that the couple had gone into the toilet to carry on their argument away from prying eyes, and as tempers rose she probably hit him and he retaliated by seizing her round the throat. The shock of this proved fatal and the court held that he had killed her, although obviously without having intended to do so.

The court took this into account in handing out a lenient sentence of just nine months' imprisonment. A niggling doubt remained in the minds of

A recent view of Leuchars station. The Inter-City 125s may now look a little outdated but they have proved to be a superb investment.

some of those affected by the young woman's death. Had the man used his knowledge of her heart condition to kill her? If this was true, it seems odd to choose the toilet compartment of a crowded train as the place to bring his relationship with the woman to such a drastic and sudden end. We shall never know.

An Appointment with Albert Pierrepoint

Railway ticket offices at small, quiet stations late at night used to be tempting targets for robbers. Nowadays most small, quiet stations do not have ticket offices at all, let alone ones that are open in the evenings.

Ash Vale, next station along the line after Aldershot going towards London Waterloo, was a small but busy station, though by eight in the evening most of the remaining passengers using the station were eagerly making their way home from London or wherever else they had been. Few of them wished to book tickets at that time of the night and so the Southern Region of British Railways as an economy measure in the 1950s closed the booking offices at stations like Ash Vale around eight in the evening. A porter then issued what few tickets might be required.

So it was that about eight in the evening on 22 August 1952 the clerk, whose name was Dean, locked up the office at Ash Vale leaving the porter the means of issuing tickets to any belated travellers who wanted them. The clerk told the porter that he would be staying in the office for an hour or more to catch up with some paperwork. About an hour later a soldier saw the light on in the office and knocked on the window whereupon the confused sounds coming from inside stopped abruptly. He knocked on the window again but received no response.

Another railwayman on his way to work saw the light on in the office, and thinking that it had been left on by mistake knocked on the door. He must have been the inquisitive sort because he then climbed up in order to look through a chink of space left by the blind. What he saw horrified him. A man's body lay on its back in a pool of blood. He could even see that the door of the small safe was open.

The unfortunate Dean had been subjected to a ferocious attack in which he had received over twenty stab wounds on his body and elsewhere. The motive had clearly been robbery because the safe was empty. Many heavy coin bags lay on the floor but about £168 was missing. The railway police and the county constabulary immediately started a murder investigation. Aldershot was close by and the military personnel stationed there were quizzed and a search was undertaken of all hotels and boarding houses in the area. This proved to be unrewarding work until a tip-off persuaded two officers to make a return visit to a multi-occupied boarding house.

Here, in a rather seedy bed-sit, they found a number of blood-stained articles – clothing and money and a passport. They waited for the occupant of the room to turn up and promptly arrested him when they did. He was caught completely by surprise and could not take the pressure. He surrendered a knife secreted in the chimney, gave them some pieces of paperwork taken from the safe at Ash Vale station and showed them his wallet which contained rather more money than a man living in such a place would normally be expected to have legitimately on his person. He also had a set of new clothes which he had clearly bought to replace those stained with the blood of the unfortunate railway clerk. There could not have been much more obvious evidence of guilt. The attacker's name was John James Alcott.

It was clear that the robbery had been some time in the planning. Alcott was a locomotive fireman and he used the fraternity so common among railway workers to make friends with and win the trust of the clerk in the ticket office at Ash Vale. His opening gambit had been to ask Dean about the times of boat trains from Victoria to Dover. He became a familiar face and in particular he used the relationship to get access to the office and, with the clerk's permission, to make short telephone calls, always, at least so he said, to other railwaymen. Clearly this was his way of casing the joint.

Over a week or two he made repeated visits to the clerk, passing the time of day over a mug of tea until the fatal evening when, although the office had closed as we have heard, the luckless Dean was catching up with the backlog. Fatally he admitted Alcott who, after a few minutes, launched a savage attack. Dean put up a good, but not good enough, fight. Alcott was sentenced to death for what was described by the judge as a 'cold-blooded murder'. Dean had been a married man with a young daughter.

It turned out that Alcott had been in trouble with the authorities before. In 1949 he was in the Coldstream Guards serving in Germany and had been sentenced to death for the murder of a German civilian but he had evaded execution on some technicality. His appointment with the famed public hangman Albert Pierrepoint was at Wandsworth Prison on Friday 2 June 1953 and was brief and one-sided.

A recent view of Ash Vale station, hardly an impressive building. It has, however, to be better than a bus shelter.

What happened at Gloucester Road Tube?

It is probably true to say that there have been remarkably few murders on the London Underground given the massive passenger usage of the system over what is now almost a century and a half since the first trains ran between Paddington and Farringdon. One twentieth-century murder has never been solved.

It occurred on 24 May 1957 at Gloucester Road on the deep-level Piccadilly Line part of the station. An aristocratic lady of Polish extraction, Teresa Lubienska, was seen by witnesses leaving a tube train but unfortunately before the day of CCTV; no one saw what happened next. She was evidently attacked and apparently stabbed many times by an unknown assailant who is thought to have escaped via the emergency staircase. Her body was found soon after she had died but no clue has ever been established as to the motive for the murder or to the identity of the murderer.

Frontage of the present-day Gloucester Road underground station. We should be pleased that some thoughtful restoration work has been carried out on this building.

Slam–door electric multiple-units of the type once so familiar in London's southern suburbs. The picture is taken at Addiscombe which no longer sees 'heavy-rail' trains but is served by the very successful Croydon Tramlink.

More Recent Crimes

We chose not to enter into detail about the more recent serious crimes to take place on Britain's railways, but crime has continued. In the 1980s, a number of young women were sexually assaulted, raped and sometimes murdered on or around railway property in the Greater London area. The reports of these attacks made many women reluctant to travel but the life of the metropolis had to go on and women of necessity continued to travel by themselves. The dual perpetrators of these crimes were apprehended and punished.

Another crime of the 1980s involved a woman travelling in the compartment of a slam-door electric multiple-unit. On the train's arrival at its destination, the woman's body was discovered having suffered multiple stab wounds. This case remains open.

The railway has also been used as a secondary tool in murder. It has been known for murderers, having killed their victims, to then place the body on a railway track in the hope that a passing train would make the death appear accidental.

CHAPTER FIVE

ASSORTED CRIME

In this chapter we take a brief look at some aspects of crime associated with the railways which are not dealt with elsewhere in the book.

A case could be made for saying that the navvies were the unsung heroes of Britain's railway revolution. They laboured in huge numbers doing the most difficult and dangerous work when over 20,000 route miles of railways were being built in the nineteenth century. It was the navvies who hewed away at solid rock making cuttings and tunnels, and it was their skilled physical efforts that enabled the building of thousands of embankments, bridges and viaducts.

The names of the big contractors such as Peto and Brassey have lived on, but those of the navvies – many of them who died or were maimed while doing this heroic work – have largely been forgotten. That the role of the navvies has to some extent become better appreciated owes much to the pioneering work of Terry Coleman, whose book *The Railway Navvies* was first published in 1965. It was aptly subtitled 'The history of the men who made the railways'. Other, later examples of this kind of history from below have expanded on and amplified what Coleman wrote.

These writers show that the blame for many of the accidents in which men died or were injured can be laid at the feet of those contractors who placed profit before the safety and welfare of their workers. They also demonstrate how the men were defrauded, often by subcontractors who frequently used the truck system to pay the men a substantial part of their wages in the form of tokens which were only redeemable at the subcontractors own shops. There they ripped the navvies off with high prices and poor-quality goods which were often underweight. Few contractors ever faced legal proceedings. There were some contractors, however, who treated their men decently.

The navvies, it has to be said, were no saints. They often came like an invading army and a large force of such men was bound to upset the relative tranquillity of remote rural settlements that were close to the path of such lines as the Settle & Carlisle and the Carlisle to Edinburgh 'Waverley Route'. The navvies frequently boasted of their drinking, eating and fighting prowess and were shunned and feared by many for their apparent godlessness. They gambled, they poached, they swore, they blasphemed and they swaggered around in their distinctive clothes. They cared not one toss for the mores of middle-class Victorian society while they looked down loftily on the ordinary labourers who did the routine jobs on the construction sites and were not part of the elite. The navvies even had women with them in their encampments who were not their wives. This scandalised respectable Victorian society!

Many of the navvies were of Irish and Scottish origin. They had a marked antipathy to the English navvies, a feeling which was heartily reciprocated. When a reason could be found, and they did not have to look hard, then the Irish fought the Scots or the English, or two of the ethnic groups would combine to fight the third. Such groupings could change overnight. Inevitably the presence of large numbers of rough, tough itinerant alpha males led to trouble – with each other and with the local police. The latter were often hopelessly outnumbered and overawed by the presence of the navvies.

The disputes, which sometimes evolved into riots, were often about concrete issues facing the navvies in their everyday work. These might involve wage rates or complaints about the truck or 'tommy-shops' and in these cases ethnic considerations usually took second place to workers' solidarity. Trouble was most frequent when the men were paid, which was sometimes only monthly and often in a pub – a mutually advantageous arrangement made between contractor and publican.

Temporarily flush with money, the navvies would embark on a monster drinking orgy which on at least one occasion ended when the pub ran out of beer and the navvies, who by this time were fighting mad, showed their disgust by literally pulling the building down. On occasions the railway contractors used navvies as soldiers in battles with landowners and their retainers, or even other contractors, a kind of strange reprise of the old days of feudalism. Examples include the 'Battles' of Saxby on the Rutland and Leicestershire border, Mickleton Tunnel in Worcestershire and Clifton Junction, north of Manchester.

It would be wrong to conclude that the navvies were a wholly lawless and nihilistic group of men. Most of their working hours and their leisure activities were, of course, carried out entirely unexceptionally. The vast majority of navvies were law-abiding for most of the time. As always from the point of view of the media the only good news was bad news, and the books written

Barrow-runs in use during the building of a deep cutting, probably on the London & Birmingham Railway in the late 1830s. A horse at the top pulled the wooden barrow up the wooden ramp, steered by the navvy, an extremely hazardous operation especially when the ramp was slippery with mud.

about them have made much of the activities that came to the attention of the authorities at the time. This has inevitably coloured popular perceptions of the navvies but the reality is that, collectively, they made an enormous contribution to the creation of Britain's railway system and therefore to the revolutionary impact that the railways had on the economy and on society.

Although the names of the individuals concerned have largely been forgotten, it is pleasant to record that at Otley in West Yorkshire and close to the parish church of All Saints there is a monument to twenty-three railway navvies. They lost their lives in the building of Bramhope Tunnel on what became known as the Leeds Northern Railway between Leeds and Northallerton. The line was opened throughout in 1849 and the tunnel was then the third longest in Britain. The monument, towards the cost of which the contractor made a substantial contribution, consists of a miniature railway tunnel with two splendidly castellated portals. Its maximum height is 6ft. It is inscribed with a number of biblical quotations but not with the names of any of those who had died.

Navvies of the 1890s, probably engaged on the building of the Great Central Railway's London Extension.

Trespass

The total number of people killed while trespassing on the railways has never been computed but records suggest that in 1843 at least seventeen died and in 1903 the remarkable figure of 442 is given. Moving trains and railway installations provided a host of hazards, but despite notices to the effect that trespassers were liable to prosecution (under criminal rather than civil law), they have and indeed continue to take risks, including using the railway as a short cut.

The memorial in Otley churchyard to the navvies who died in the building of the nearby Bramhope Tunnel.

In the earliest days of the railways people seemed to find it hard to appreciate that if a train was bearing down on them it could not swerve to avoid hitting them unlike a horse and rider or a horse-drawn wagon or carriage. It would be futile to attempt to identify all the reasons why trespass has taken place, but it often occurred when some other offence was being perpetrated such as theft of railway property or poaching.

Drunks often took short cuts along railway lines, endangering themselves as well as others. In 1844 at Hebden Bridge in the old West Riding of Yorkshire a man was found asleep right by the railway track, his head only inches from the rail. Such was the depth of his drunken slumbers that at least two trains had passed on this particular track, one of which had knocked his hat off, without him awakening. The courts have not generally been very understanding where befuddled and confused passengers have trespassed, even if they did so unconsciously.

In 1864 a company generally known as the Solway Junction Railway was established with the intention of moving iron ore from West Cumberland to the iron and steel works in Lanarkshire in Scotland. To provide a short route independent of rival companies the decision was taken to build a viaduct from just south of Annan on the Scottish side to Bowness on the English shore across the notoriously dangerous waters of the Solway Firth. The Solway Viaduct was a rather flimsy-looking structure no less than 1,940yds long and carried on 193 cast-iron piers. It opened fully for traffic in 1870.

This long-forgotten viaduct proved to be something of a white elephant because the high-quality Cumberland haematite ore was mostly worked out by the end of the century. It also proved expensive to maintain because the piers were scoured by the unpredictable currents in the firth, and in cold winters substantial ice floes came down the Solway hitting and seriously damaging the structure.

The few remaining trains were withdrawn in 1921 and the viaduct was left to its own devices. It was demolished between 1933 and 1935 and the only traffic in the final years had been doughty, determined and thirsty Scotsmen who trespassed by walking across the increasingly decrepit viaduct so that they could enjoy a few drinks in the English pubs on a Sunday, their own being closed on that day.

To walk across the viaduct was no mean undertaking on account of its exposure to howling winds and spray thrown up by the turbulent waters of the firth and its increasingly unsafe condition. Eventually a watchman was employed at the southern end to stop trespass but it was found easy to bribe him with a bottle or two which made his lonely vigil a little more bearable. Generations of trainspotters systematically trespassed when entering locomotive sheds and works in pursuit of engine numbers. These places were quite extraordinarily hazardous and even more so at night when spotters felt they were less likely to be seen. Some sheds attracted spotters, or 'gricers' as they were sometimes known, in huge numbers and staff were forced to spend much of their time in a futile attempt to keep them out.

At some sheds this was like trying to plug a collapsing dam with a finger and staff simply gave up, disgusted by the antics of those who regarded themselves as railway enthusiasts. Occasionally they or the railway police caught a few youths and gave them a good talking to. In the 1950s and 1960s this might have given them sufficient enough a scare to act as a deterrent… until the next time. At some of the most sought-after and well-guarded sheds, Crewe North comes to mind, the spotters would gather in a group of thirty or more

The Solway Viaduct. The approach embankment to this lonely and ill-fated viaduct can be still seen on the English side of the Solway Firth not far from Bowness-on-Solway.

and storm their way into the shed on the basis that they could not all be caught, and that between them they would manage to note down all the numbers, including those in the shed's inner recesses. Such a stampede was almost impossible to prevent.

Elsewhere great ingenuity might be employed in gaining access to the hallowed portals of a shed. Spotters might squat down so that they could not be seen by the foreman as they shuffled surreptitiously past the office window at the entrance, or they might hide out of view behind a moving engine and gain access that way. Holes in fences, a scuttle across a convenient roof or even climbing a tree and dropping from a well-placed branch – these and a host of other methods were employed in the attempt to gain entry and secure some more 'cops' to put in the treasured *ABC*.

Notices warning against trespass were studiously ignored and it was known that few trespassing spotters were ever actually taken to court. Even live electric conductor rails such as those in the vicinity of a Gateshead shed on Tyneside were not enough to deter some of the more determined, or should we say foolhardy, spotters. It was a risk they were prepared to take to be able to enter those elusive numbers in their books.

One of the most serious cases of trespass occurred on the evening of 23 May 1970 on the Britannia Bridge across the Menai Strait between the Welsh mainland and Anglesey. This remarkable piece of engineering was designed by Robert Stephenson for the Chester & Holyhead Railway and opened in 1850. It consisted of two masonry piers supporting four rectangular wrought iron tubes through which the trains ran. In fact it was a larger and more sophisticated version of Stephenson's other tubular bridge at Conwy.

Two boys climbed onto the bridge. They may or may not have been looking for birds' nests or for bats but because it was dark they made impromptu torches out of burning paper. Pieces of burning paper ignited oil and creosote deposits and collections of dried leaves, and quickly the tubes became an inferno. They

No.46256 *Sir William Stanier* F.R.S and its companion No.46257 *City of Salford* were refinements of the original 'Coronation' Pacifics designed by Stanier for the London, Midland & Scottish Railway in the late 1930s. They were built in 1947, and for many enthusiasts represent the apogee of British steam express passenger locomotive design development. When No.46256 was withdrawn for scrapping, it was still in first-class running order. Crewe North Shed is the location.

were damaged beyond reasonable repair and for a while it looked as if the line to Holyhead which crossed the bridge might have to be closed permanently. Eventually the bridge was reconstructed without the tubes and as a double-decker bridge with the A55 road running above the railway.

A Peeping Tom

In 1954 an engine driver and his younger fireman mate had worked a freight train from Buxton to Hooton in the Wirral where they were relieved, a new crew taking it on the last stage of its journey to Birkenhead only a few miles down the line. The men were then due to travel back 'on the cushions' – railway parlance for travelling in the comfort of a passenger train. It was not always a quick and easy journey for such enginemen to get back to their home depot although it helped that they were being paid for doing so.

Sometimes control would come through with an instruction that there was another job for them – working a train back towards their own depot, but no such unwelcome message was received and it was with some relief that the duo caught a local train to Rock Ferry, where they transferred to an electric train which took them under the River Mersey and to the low level plat-forms at Liverpool Central. At the high level platforms of Liverpool Central they were due to catch a train to Warrington and, having checked that control had not found them a job, they settled down in a compartment on a late evening train destined for Manchester Central.

The train was made up of what were then suburban-style compartment coaches hauled by a Stanier 2-6-4 tank engine. These carriages had tradi-tional slam doors and bench seats facing each other across the width of the coach. The fireman sat by the door on the off side of the carriage, facing the direction of travel. The driver was the only other occupant of the compart-ment. The train puffed out of Liverpool Central and plunged into a series of gloomy, soot-encrusted tunnels and cuttings before emerging into the open air at Brunswick with a brief view of the southern end of Liverpool's long dockland waterfront.

At this point it was still possible at that time to glimpse a three-car train on Liverpool's famous Overhead Railway. Even at night these made a great spectacle. On this occasion, however, the driver could not spare a thought for the view, because even before the train had emerged into the open air he said that there was the sound of smashing glass and a large hole appeared in the window by his mate's head. The fireman, he said, was unconscious and his head was bleeding badly.

He presumed that some heavy object had been thrown and the result was the injury to his mate. The driver pulled the communication cord and the train came to a halt at St Michael's station. An ambulance was called and the unfortunate fireman, still unconscious, was rushed to hospital but pronounced dead on arrival. The police were called in to investigate. There had been a spate of stone-throwing on this section of line but this time throwing stones had led to a death. Or had it?

The carriage and the compartment were closely examined by the police and it was immediately confirmed that the carriage window had indeed been broken from the outside, but where was the missile involved? It certainly was not to be seen inside the compartment. So where was it? Then bloodstains were found on the **outside** of the carriage. The line in the vicinity of the incident was searched immediately.

The Britannia Bridge over the Menai Straits soon after opening. Although the picture is incorrect in many details, it gives a good idea of the tubes through which the trains passed.

A recent view of the Britannia Bridge in its current form with the tubes removed and the road carried above the railway.

At this particular point there were three tracks, two for running purposes and one in the middle which usually contained empty passenger carriages. Fragments of bone and small pieces of broken glass lay on the ballast at the Liverpool end of a rake of carriages in this siding. Closer examination revealed that the guard's small lookout window on the empty end carriage was broken. Human hairs were adhering to it. Could the driver's explanation of what happened be a lie?

The compartment was examined very closely and bloodstains were found on the light bulb along with a fingerprint. It was clear that the bulb had first been removed and then replaced, most likely after the fireman had received his fatal injury. The rolling stock in the middle track was then subjected to close examination. A blood smear could be seen along the side of two of the coaches facing the side of the carriage where the fireman had allegedly been sitting.

Had the driver and the fireman been engaged in a desperate hand-to-hand struggle as a result of which the fireman had been pushed out of the open window so far that his head had come into collision with the empty rolling stock on the adjacent line? Had his head then broken the window before he was hauled back into the compartment and the driver pulled the communication cord? Was there some dire feud between the two men? Why had the light bulb been removed and then replaced? The fingerprints of both men were on it. A theory of what actually happened was beginning to form itself in the minds of the investigating officers.

They thought that the idea of such a fight was unlikely although they did not summarily dismiss it. However, what if the fireman had been engaged in 'dogging' with the active assistance of the driver? Those who practised this particular form of sexual voyeurism usually did so at night having entered a compartment in a non-corridor coach and previously ascertained that the adjacent compartment was occupied by a young couple. They would remove the light bulb in their own compartment and then lean as far out of the window as they dared in order to see whether the couple were engaged in sexual activity. On this particular line both participants would have needed to 'move quickly' between stations, most of which were only about five minutes apart.

The driver admitted that his mate had indeed been dogging, although he went to great lengths to say that he himself had not been involved. The likely scenario was that the fireman had removed the light bulb and then leaned out of the window with the driver hanging on to his legs. When he leaned out too far he had come into collision with the guard's van of the empty stock and the driver had then pulled him back into the compartment, pushed him into the seat, used a hand lamp to locate the light bulb, replaced it and then pulled the communication cord. A verdict of misadventure was passed on the deceased fireman.

Railways and the Chartists

Some luminary once said that politics is distilled economics. If economics is the study of the production, exchange, distribution and consumption of wealth, then perhaps politics could be characterised as the arguments concerning how that wealth and the power that goes with it should be shared out. If this is so it is not surprising that the railways have found themselves embroiled in political activity, and that sometimes that activity has broken the law of the land.

The economic, social and political impact of the Industrial Revolution in Britain has been endlessly studied. It involved a staggering increase in the wealth-producing capacity of manufacturing, mining and other business enterprises and was accompanied by a remarkable rise in the productivity and output of agriculture. Few people question that, over time, it led to a large rise in the living standards and expectations of the mass of the population. There was, however, a substantial human cost with the 'tyranny of the clock', brutal discipline in the workplace and with the creation of overcrowded, insanitary and polluted industrial settlements. The shared experience of working people led them to realise that the only means for them to improve their situation was through collective action.

Trade unions developed out of this experience as did the Chartist movement from the mid-1830s to the early 1850s. The Chartist movement could be described as the first political party of the working classes. It campaigned vigorously for a programme of reforms that it believed would enable Parliament to meet the needs and aspirations of ordinary people. Chartism was a broad and complex movement, a catch-all expression for a wide range of discontents and grievances and it embraced some who believed only in the methods of peaceful persuasion, those who were prepared to resort to armed struggle and others who were prepared to consider the use of both types of tactic depending on circumstances.

The Chartist movement was genuinely national but its support was largely to be found in and around industrial towns, large and small. Chartist meetings could attract mass audiences whose anger might be aroused by passionate speakers and this could threaten the maintenance of law and order. The authorities took the Chartist movement very seriously, at least when it was enjoying its peaks of popularity, and felt that, when and where it was deemed necessary, the State should make a show of force to discourage the insurrectionary tendencies that were always felt to be lurking under the surface when large numbers of disaffected working class and lower-middle class people got together.

The railways not only assisted Chartist speakers to travel around perfectly legally, addressing meetings up and down the country, but they could also be used to move troops far more quickly and easily to potential trouble spots than had previously been possible. In 1839, for example, trouble was expected at a

Chartist meeting at Coventry and the London & Birmingham Railway was used to transport a force of soldiers from Birmingham in double-quick time.

A large central barracks had been built at Weedon in Northamptonshire in 1803 and this was extended, partly because its position close to what became the West Coast Main Line made it ideal as the point of despatch of troops quickly by train. Other barracks were established especially in the north of England with the same purpose in mind.

Charlie Peace

Passenger trains were also used to convey prisoners under guard, a practice not relished by the majority of other travellers or, possibly, by railway employees, not least because on a few occasions such prisoners managed to escape, causing chaos in and around railway installations.

One such prisoner was the celebrated Charlie Peace. He was the proud possessor of an extremely impressive criminal curriculum vitae, so multi-faceted that it is impossible to do justice to it here. Much of his criminal activity consisted of audacious and highly skilled burglaries, which he often undertook in masterful disguises. He was a cat burglar or, as they called them so delightfully in those days, a 'portico thief'. He was a compulsive and very successful philanderer but his relentless pursuit of the female sex led inevitably to considerable complications.

It was perhaps these complications that meant that Peace began to lose his grip, and having previously eschewed violence, turned to murder. In 1879 he was being brought from London to stand trial for a murder committed in Sheffield and was accompanied by two burly police officers in a reserved compartment of a Great Northern Railway train. Peace, despite being phenomenally ugly, could charm the birds off the trees, and he set about winning the confidence of these two officers. He was so plausible that after a couple of hours they undid his handcuffs.

By this time the train had passed Worksop and Peace knew that he had to move quickly. When they least expected it Peace made a jump for the door, opened it and tried to leap out. Unfortunately for him the more alert of the two officers grabbed his foot and refused to let go. The train was travelling quickly and anyone watching from the line-side would have been treated to the sight of Peace dangling out the carriage, his foot in the vice-like grip of the police officer and his body banging to and fro against the carriage side as the train sped along.

Perhaps the officers were too intent on trying not to let Peace go that it was a couple of miles before they got round to pulling the communication cord. With a desperate twist of his foot Peace managed to wriggle out of his shoe and drop to the ground, whereupon he slid down an embankment sustaining various injuries. He was quickly recaptured and atoned for his sins by being hanged in February 1879. The world became a better – if less colourful – place

A Chartist meeting at Kennington Common. Chartist speakers made considerable use of railways as they stomped around the country addressing meetings, usually in the open air.

the day that Charlie Peace died. It is interesting to note that Peace had broken free at Darnall. This eastern suburb of Sheffield was where he had once told people he wanted to be buried. Quite why Darnall should be honoured in this way is not obvious. It is not the most attractive of Sheffield's suburbs!

Railways and Prize Fights

A little-known and curious misuse of railway facilities back in the nineteenth century was that of conveying passengers to prize fights. A number of long-standing recreational activities such as bear-baiting, bull-running and bare-knuckle boxing came to be thought of as immoral and barbaric under pressure from the rising middle-classes and the Evangelical movement in the Church of England. However, from the early eighteenth century through to the second half of the nineteenth, pugilism, as it was often called, enjoyed great popularity.

The contestants fought without any protection for their hands and could inflict appalling injuries on each other, deaths not being unknown. The leading fighters, men like Bendigo, Mendoza, Tom Cribb and Ben Caunt, could become rich. The major contests attracted enormous crowds who were often drunk and fiercely partisan, so much so that the supporters of the contestants frequently fought each other. They also became feverishly excited because of the number and value of the bets that were placed. They therefore posed a threat to public order and the magistrates, ever fearful of large assemblies of working people with their passions aroused, frequently banned the contests.

With so much money at stake, however, the organisers often connived with the railway companies to outthink the authorities and set up a contest in some secret and remote place, such as a natural hollow preferably hidden from the authorities. Special trains were laid on but the arrangements had to be kept as secret as possible until the very last minute. Often the driver had no idea where the train was going until it was time to set off and he opened a sealed package containing his instructions! The first such 'pugilism special' seems to have been that which carried passengers from London Bridge to Horley in February 1844. The railway companies did very well out of them until this 'sporting activity' went out of fashion a couple of decades later.

A bare-knuckle boxing bout in the eighteenth century. Pugilism still attracted large crowds in the nineteenth, and when it was banned some railway companies put on clandestine specials. The fights were staged deep in the country and the arrangements kept secret until the last possible minute.

CHAPTER SIX

THE WORK OF THE
TRANSPORT POLICE

The British took a long time to be won to the idea of a professional police force. This was because of concerns that such a force would intrude not only into criminal activities but also into the private and political aspects of people's lives as it was widely believed occurred with such forces in France, for example. However, the development of large-scale industrialisation in Britain was accompanied by interrelated processes involving a rapid expansion in the size of the economy, significant population growth and urbanisation.

One result was an increase in the opportunities for criminal activity, especially among the volatile population of the rapidly growing towns. Much of the growing population consisted of people who had migrated from elsewhere on the mainland or from Ireland and they frequently lacked the social and familial ties of the long-established communities from which they had come. They also tended to lack deference to such traditional sources of authority as the big local landowner or the established Church.

For several generations society in the developing towns and cities was in a state of considerable turmoil as a response to the immense tensions created by the twin processes of industrialisation and urbanisation. Although statistics relating to the eighteenth century are very incomplete, it is clear that there was a considerable increase in all sorts of crime and that the existing, largely amateur, methods of maintaining law and order were incapable of keeping this increase under control.

Nowhere was this more true than London and it was in the metropolis that the progenitors of modern professional policing can be found. The famous Bow Street Runners had been set up in 1750 and they were largely paid only when their activity led to the successful prosecution of wrong-doers. In this sense they were bounty-hunters or thief-takers. Such men had a long history in Britain. Various mounted and foot patrols were established over the next decades, also under the control of the Bow Street magistrates.

The Pool of London, with its vast amounts of shipping and enormous diversity of valuable cargoes in the holds of ships or on neighbouring quaysides and in warehouses, attracted thieves like moths to a flame, and the result was that tens of millions of pounds worth of goods went missing annually. In an attempt to stem this flow the Thames River Police were formed by an Act of Parliament in 1800. This was a regular professional police force. Similar but far better known were the Metropolitan Police who were established by law in 1829 as a result of the continuing efforts of the then Home Secretary, Sir Robert Peel. The success of the 'Bobbies' or 'Peelers' led to the creation of similar forces elsewhere over the next decades, and it was not long before the establishment of such constabularies became mandatory in England and Wales.

The first railway company to employ men in a police role was the Stockton & Darlington which opened in 1825. Their brief was to guard the railway and its associated activities against theft and other crime, to patrol as a visible deterrent to potential criminal activity and to contribute to the safe working of the line. They were full-time paid employees and were dressed distinctively in a uniform of a non-military style.

The more significant Liverpool & Manchester Railway opened in 1830 and had a police force with similar duties, except that additionally they acted as the predecessors of signalmen — or signallers as they are now called. It was this role, in combination with their uniforms which were modelled on those of the Metropolitan Police, that led to railway workers using the word 'Bobby' to refer to signalmen. The early railway policemen only had powers of arrest on railway property itself and were frequently left impotently cursing their ill luck when a suspect was sufficiently fleet of foot to evade their clutches and escape onto adjoining land.

In 1838 railway companies were required by law to provide their own police forces instead of drawing on local constabularies. This had been something which ratepayers strongly resented because they did not see why they should subsidise the security needs of private companies. The boisterous and some-times illegal activities of the railway navvies have been discussed elsewhere, but they required a lot of policing and local forces had often been called upon to keep order, the numbers of railway company police often being insufficient to cope with outbreaks of trouble.

A number of towns, of which Crewe, Swindon and Wolverton are examples, were virtually created by the railways and were company towns in that sense. There the railway police in the early days carried out the functions of the county constabulary where such a force existed. One by one the railway companies established their own police forces and the men concerned were faced with an intimidating set of duties. Let us take the regulations of the Great Western Railway as an example.

Apart from the overall requirement that the police officers be vigilant and watch over and preserve law and order on railway property, they had to receive and despatch signals, operate points and crossings, ensure there were no obstructions on the line, assist in the event of accidents, remove trespassers, patrol lines and installations to ensure that all the company workers were carrying out their duties satisfactorily, announce arrivals and departures, provide help and information for people requiring assistance, watch for such possibilities as land slips or bridge failures, make safety checks on the rails and sleepers and ensure that their superior officers were kept fully up-to-date with all developments and incidents.

When required they were expected to carry passengers' luggage and check tickets. In return for this they received a wage, in most cases unlikely to exceed one pound for a six-day week. Fortunately this range of duties gradually became curtailed as they tended to be taken over by specialist workers and the officers were able to concentrate on what Gilbert and Sullivan described as constabulary duties. Oh yes, they were also expected to salute passing trains!

Another aspect of railway policing was detective work and, of course, you've guessed it, as if the poor old railway bobby was not busy enough already he was expected to do a spot of detecting as well. However, it was not long before specialist detectives began to be used. They worked in plain clothes and were often disguised as porters or similar staff and they worked inconspicuously on stations and in goods depots where thefts were regularly taking place.

Perhaps a more interesting job was following and watching people who had made large claims for compensation from a railway company for personal injuries supposedly sustained on or around railway property. It was by no means unknown for such people to obtain the necessary medical certification and yet to be seen striding purposefully – and with a look of eager greedy anticipation – towards the courtroom where their case was about to be considered. They did not always have the sense to slow down and start limping when they came in sight of the court!

One example of such a fraudster was a passenger aboard a train of the London & North Western Railway which received a slight bump during a shunting operation at Euston station. It really was only the slightest jolt and no one else bothered except this particular gentleman, who claimed that he had not only had an awful shock but he had also injured his back so severely that he was unable to carry on his lucrative private business. He demanded compensation. It was quickly discovered that the man had no business at all but was in serious debt and had chanced on the incident at Euston as a way of raising much-needed cash.

A railway policeman indicating the 'All Clear'. His general appearance is like the Metropolitan Police established around 1829 by Sir Robert Peel.

He was trailed for several weeks by railway detectives who watched him as he heaved great pieces of furniture and heavy trunks and boxes around when helping a lady friend to move home. He was also seen romping energetically on the floor with the lady's infant son. His case against the company was summarily dismissed by the court and the London & North Western Railway then took out a warrant for perjury. Our friend had managed to scrape together sufficient money for a ticket to the USA but he was arrested shortly before he was due to embark. His reward was nine months' hard labour.

Perhaps typical of the thousand and one seemingly mundane cases dealt with by the railway detectives was one which came to court at Birmingham in 1917. In the dock was James Hardwick, a shunter in the employment of the Great Western Railway and he was accused of having stolen half a pint of essence of lemonade to the value of one shilling from a box van at Hockley Goods Depot in the city. Two Great Western Railway detectives were on the night shift at the depot and heard someone moving around in the van. They squatted down and awaited developments.

It was Hardwick in the van and he was apprehended carrying a drinking can containing lemonade, which he said he had been using to put under a leaking container of the drink. There was indeed a large stone jar containing essence of lemonade in the van but it was not leaking. There were also containers of whisky and the court took the somewhat uncharitable view that Hardwick, and perhaps others, were helping themselves to the odd whisky and lemonade to make the night shift a little more tolerable.

Hardwick was fined but managed to avoid a custodial sentence. It is likely that he also lost his job. A very different incident occurred in the 1900s at what was then Cardiff general station. There a Great Western Railway detective intervened in the nick of time to prevent a dastardly Frenchman eloping with an eighteen-year-old Welsh girl described as being 'of exceedingly attractive appearance'.

Sometimes the activities of the railway police provided a bit of knockabout farce. Early in the 1980s plain-clothes officers were investigating a series of ingenious thefts of mail bags from railway property at Basingstoke. They kept watch on the platform and, to their surprise, saw what looked like a clerical gentleman making off with a number of mail bags. They gave chase and apprehended the man only to be set upon in turn by two robust elderly ladies who belaboured the officers with their umbrellas, convinced that the clergyman was being assaulted by cowardly thugs. The 'clerical gentleman' turned out to be a professional actor between jobs whose brief criminal career around Basingstoke station had garnered him about £100,000 of stolen mail.

In the 1980s the police, including British Transport Police, were aware that a very dangerous vagrant was at large, with a string of convictions for drink-related offences and who had previously been tried and acquitted on a murder and attempted murder charge. He had confessed to an officer that he had killed at least nine people and attacked innumerable others, his victims always fellow vagrants for whom he had enormous contempt.

A conviction was very hard to bring about, the vagrants being reluctant to help the police with enquiries, but eventually, after killing again, the perpetrator was charged and stood trial. He received two life sentences, the judge commenting that he showed no remorse and had to be kept behind walls because he posed such a danger to the public.

The Transport Police were involved again in that decade when the body of a young man was found beside a railway line in south London. The man was known to be gay and so officers went undercover to investigate, assisted by a witness. Luckily, after the body of another man was found, this witness was able to identify the attacker. The man concerned confessed to these and further crimes and was convicted.

Another criminal activity which British Transport Police or their predecessors have had to deal with is terrorism. It has a long history. In the
1860s and 1880s a number of incidents involved the Fenians who were
Irish nationalists. Those in the 1880s were serious. In January 1883 some
explosions caused damage at a number of locations around Glasgow
including Buchanan Street Goods Depot. In October 1883 there were
explosions on the London Underground at the then Praed Street station
and later between Charing Cross and Westminster. Fortunately there were
no fatalities.

Various bomb scares caused considerable disruption and a large bomb
caused significant damage at London's Victoria station on 26 February 1884.
A Metropolitan Railway train travelling from Aldgate to Hammersmith
was bombed near Gower Street station (now Euston Square), but the
damage was spectacular rather than lethal. Searches by railway police of
the cloakrooms of all the main termini in London revealed three other
bombs. Hidden in a case, each bomb consisted of a detonating device
embedded in dynamite and primed to go off at a predetermined time.
They were skilfully disarmed. A sustained campaign by the police led to
many arrests and by 1885 it was clear that this particular bombing campaign was over.

There have been sporadic outbreaks of terrorist activity on the railways
since that time. Here are some examples. The Irish Republican Army (IRA)
exploded a number of bombs mostly around London and Birmingham in
1939 and 1940, and the Provisional IRA gave notice of its intentions in 1973
when there were explosions at London's King's Cross and Euston stations
which injured twenty-one people. 1976 saw a bomb demolish most of a carriage on a train leaving Cannon Street station in London. Fortunately this was
an empty stock train and it suggests that whoever planted the bomb got the
timing wrong.

Only a few days later a terrorist got onto a train at West Ham underground
station carrying a bomb secreted in a briefcase. It was not secreted very well
because the briefcase began to emit smoke. The terrorist panicked and threw
the briefcase down the carriage whereupon it exploded causing many injuries. The terrorist himself was hurt, but in trying to get away shot and killed a
policeman before being shot himself.

'Genuine' warnings of bombs and hoaxes can also cause just the kind
of confusion and disruption that warms the heart of a terrorist. Suspect
packages left in strategic places can work wonders in bringing transport systems to a grinding halt. Thirty-nine potentially explosive and/or incendiary
devices were found close to lines used by passenger trains between February
1991 and October 1994 alone. Most were in Greater London. Not all were
actually capable of being detonated but in some cases were probably placed

with the intention of causing disruption rather than destruction, injury or death.

In 1990 there was a shooting at Lichfield City station when the IRA 'executed' one soldier and injured two others. In 1991 a bomb went off at Victoria and one person was killed while a bomb at London Bridge in 1992 caused twenty-nine to be injured. In July 2005 a gang of British-born Muslim suicide bombers detonated a number of bombs on the London Underground as a result of which fifty-six people died and 700 were injured.

The main-line railways and the underground are very vulnerable to the activities of terrorists, either by causing disruption, damage or death and injury, but the Transport Police have a formidable array of security devices at their disposal which can help to counter the possibility of such atrocities being repeated. Even those fairly limited political rights enjoyed by the people of Britain did not come without hard-fought campaigns and struggles which often involved recourse to illegal activity.

During the nineteenth century, and often as a result of extra-Parliamentary political methods, the majority of men gained the franchise in national and then local government elections. Many women saw no reason why they should not also be enfranchised and movements for votes and for other aspects of female emancipation built-up steadily during the nineteenth century and in the period leading up to the First World War. The attitude of many men to political rights for women was one of contemptuous dismissal and it was out of a feeling of continuing frustration with this rejection that some women turned to more extreme methods of persuasion.

These activists, often termed 'suffragettes', were prepared to employ arson and other illegal methods to draw attention to their cause. Railways were among the institutions that were on the receiving end of suffragette action in the period between December 1912 and May 1914. Railway buildings and rolling stock were vandalised and set on fire, signalling equipment tampered with and even small home-made bombs were detonated. Some failed to explode. On most occasions items were found nearby left by the suffragettes announcing that such actions would only stop once women had won the vote.

The locations of these incidents were genuinely nationwide and by no means restricted to London and the major urban areas. The furthest north incident was at Leuchars Junction on the North British Railway but the rural fastnesses of Monmouthshire were also involved. The terrorist activity ceased abruptly once war broke out because most of the suffragettes, perhaps to many people's surprise, threw themselves into support of the war effort.

A suffragette selling papers. The force-feeding of suffragettes in prison was an emotive issue which aroused both sympathy and antipathy.

An issue that had exercised the attention of the railway police from earliest times is that of vandalism. No sooner had trains started running than people began to throw missiles at them or put obstructions on the line in order to see what happened when trains hit them. Within weeks of the opening of the Liverpool & Manchester Railway in 1830 a man was arrested and fined for having placed a sleeper on the line. Many small boys, and even indeed older men who should have known better, found they could not resist the idea of standing on bridges and trying to drop stones down the chimneys of steam locomotives passing underneath. Sometimes much heavier objects were dropped on trains such as coping stones dislodged from bridges across the track. As early as 1883 when Frederick S. Williams published *Our Iron Roads* he had noted:

> ...the amount of loss which railway companies sustain from wilful and wanton damage is as great as it is inexcusable. A railway carriage is often so mutilated that it has to be upholstered de novo; and brainless fops who wear diamond rings consider it a display at once of their elegance and wit to scrape the glass in such a way as to interrupt the view, or even to outrage decency...

People have even obtained 'fun' from shooting at trains. In 1963 at Keynsham on the line between Bristol and Bath a train was hit by a flaming arrow made of copper rod during a spate of such incidents involving other targets in the area. Obviously such activities not only endangered life but also frequently damaged rolling stock and caused serious disruption.

The leather straps which were once used to close carriage windows or to adjust how far the window was open were attractive to thieves and vandals. They were made of high-quality leather and were very useful for stropping razors. Light bulbs have been removed, probably to the extent of millions over the years, and carriage seats slashed with sadistic glee. Trains have been set on fire and line-side installations such as signals, signal boxes, permanent way cabins, goods depots and passenger stations attacked and damaged. These installations have often been targeted at quiet times and have frequently been in remote locations and therefore detection by the railway police let alone prosecution has often been difficult.

It has to be said that the railways have all too often provided vandals with tempting items to place on railway lines. These include rail chairs, sleepers, concrete blocks, trolley wheel sets and other items of infrastructure liberally scattered close to running lines. However, items used in an attempt to derail a train do not necessarily have to be close to hand. In 1957 on the London, Tilbury & Southend section of the Eastern Region near Pitsea, a tree trunk weighing three hundredweight had been dragged half a mile before being placed on the line.

A cartoon of 1865. The guard pokes his head through the carriage window. 'Smoking not allowed, gents.' The swell replies, 'What's the fine?' Guard: 'A shilling, ready money to the guard, sir. Forty shillings to the company, payable by instalments at your own convenience.' Victorian humour can seem heavy-handed.

Fatalities have occurred as the result of obstructions being placed on the line deliberately. An early example was in 1851 when a train from Brighton to Lewes came off the track after hitting a sleeper which had been placed close to the line with malicious intent. The train hit a bridge parapet and tumbled down an embankment. Five people died.

The work of the British Transport Police is continuous and every day brings surprises.

CHAPTER SEVEN

CRIME AND THE RAILWAY IN FILM AND LITERATURE

'All sorts of comedy, tragedy, gallantry and melodrama of real life were often enacted in very ordinary railway compartments' wrote C. Hamilton Ellis in *Railway Carriages in the British Isles, from 1830 to 1914* (1965). The carriage was just one element of railways, but a particularly useful one that was employed widely in film and literary fiction. Additionally, railways offered a whole new range of locations such as waiting rooms, tunnels, signal boxes, sidings and stations, all of which could be readily adapted as the settings for foul and dastardly deeds. The arrival of the railway very quickly offered up a scenario with almost limitless possibilities for the writers of fiction and again for the early moving-picture makers. A relationship between the railways and the literary and cinematic arts developed which continues to this day.

That involving film began in December 1895 when the first motion picture, *The Arrival of a Train at La Ciotat Station*, was shown in Paris to an invited audience. The film, by the Lumière brothers, showed a train pulling into a station, and although the theme was simple enough it caused the audience to duck behind their seats for fear that they might be run over. Given that the crime genre had long been popular in literature it was inevitable that it would be adapted successfully for the medium of film. The railways have provided an ideal setting for books and films dealing with murder, robbery and intrigue such as *Murder on the Orient Express* (1974) and *The Lady Vanishes* (1938 and 1979).

Although these and many other films are set in Europe, the latter part of this chapter will focus on a selection of films set in Britain. We begin with what can only be a selective survey of literature dealing with railway crime.

Industrial change, the growth of towns and a rapid increase in population brought a new kind of anxiety about crime during the nineteenth century. Widening opportunities for theft opened up with rich and poor living in very close proximity and with the greater quantity and visibility of goods and materials that were available for the criminal to steal. The railways themselves offered all kinds of new possibilities for criminal activity and this was quickly reflected in fictional literature. Only a small amount of Victorian crime fiction is still read but the Sherlock Holmes stories, mainly set in the late nineteenth century (although most were written in the twentieth century), have retained their popularity and are probably the most widely known.

Crime fiction dates back before 1800 but in the nineteenth century crime writing began to aim at a mass market. The *Newgate Calendar* of the eighteenth century gave accounts of the lives and crimes of those felons condemned and executed at Newgate. It was prefaced with a moral warning about the consequence of committing the deeds that brought the wretches to such a pretty pass. However, these accounts gave way to fictional crime stories which began to give less attention to the criminal and more to those who caught them.

The earliest recognised detective story is Edgar Allen Poe's *Murders on the Rue Morgue* (1841) first published in *Graham's Magazine*. The title of the pioneering British literary detective novel (some might suggest William Godwin's *Caleb Williams* of 1794 although its plot bears little resemblance to detective fiction as we understand it) is credited to Charles Dickens' *Bleak House* (1852). Although the detective, Inspector Bucket, solves a murder, it is only a small part of a much bigger story. Crime was given a prominent role in Dickens' earlier novel, *Oliver Twist* (1837–39).

It was in the 1860s that the 'sensational novel' came to prominence in the works of writers such as Mary Elizabeth Braddon and Wilkie Collins. By the later years of the nineteenth century, crime and detective fiction as a genre had become established and was very popular, notably in the form of the short story. Dick Donovan, 'the Glasgow Detective', was a pseudonym used by Joyce Emmerson Preston Muddock (1842-1934) who wrote nearly three hundred detective and mystery stories between 1889 and 1922. Although like Sherlock Holmes, Donovan appeared in the *Strand* in 1892, he was already a well-established popular detective. His exploits featured a number of encounters with trains while engaged in chasing murderers or mail-train robbers. Following in the Victorians' footsteps were other writers like G.K. Chesterton, Arthur Morrison, R. Austin Freeman, Agatha Christie, Dorothy L. Sayers, and Margery Allingham.

Despite, or even perhaps because of, a certain literary snobbishness towards the genre, the popularity of crime fiction has long been reflected in the sales of such books on railway station bookstalls and newsagents. Victorian writers soon began to utilise the railway as a setting or backdrop to a story. Charles

Agatha Christie, the doyen of
the British murder and detection
story. Railways feature in
several of her stories. She was
born at Torquay in 1870 and is
commemorated by this plaque at
nearby Torre Abbey.

Dickens was one of the earliest and he included trains in his writings from
the 1840s. In his book *Railways and Culture in Britain* (2001), Ian Carter posed
the question of why detective fiction and Britain's railways went together like
bacon and eggs, and suggested that with 'railways enjoying a monopoly in
passenger land transport beyond the strictly local, any British writer setting a
crime story among travellers between 1830 and 1914 had little option but to
describe railway travel'.

Even if a crime did not always take place on a train, railways often entered
the story as a means of conveying the sleuth to the scene of the offence or
as a possible escape route for the perpetrator of the crime. The confines of
the old-fashioned compartment; the later possibilities afforded by corridors
and connections between carriages; the environs of stations and the minatory
gloom of railway tunnels provided a galaxy of scenarios around which to
weave a good tale.

Despite his stories containing a number of mistakes about the operations of
the railways, Sir Arthur Conan Doyle (1859-1930) featured trains in several
of his immortal Sherlock Holmes adventures. In *Silver Blaze* Holmes and
Dr Watson are on a journey to King's Pyland in Dartmoor to investigate a
murder and the disappearance of the racehorse 'Silver Blaze'. Whilst on the

Crime-writers and film-makers have not been slow to exploit the opportunities to set scenes of skulduggery in railway tunnels. This is Clay Cross tunnel in Derbyshire, opened in 1840 on the then North Midland Railway. It is over a mile long. Note the castellated entrance. Early railway travellers were often nervous about tunnels and so engineers sometimes provided castle-like features to give a sense of solidity and permanence.

train Holmes, who is looking out the window and glancing at his watch, comments casually to the faithful Watson 'We are going well... our rate at present is fifty-three and a half miles an hour... the telegraph posts upon this line are sixty yards apart, and the calculation is a simple one.'

Railway carriages provide a means whereby the mercurial Holmes can analyse and make his preparations for the case ahead as he travels on his way to solve it. In *The Boscombe Valley Mystery*, Holmes and Watson 'leave Paddington by the 11.15' to travel to rural Herefordshire. As they boarded they had the compartment to themselves where Holmes could peruse the 'immense litter of papers [he] had brought with him. Among these he rummaged and read, with intervals of note-taking and of meditation, until we were past Reading'.

Sherlock Holmes and Dr Watson sally forth by train to solve the mystery of 'Silver Blaze'. The artist, Sidney Pagett, did much to create the popular image of Sherlock Holmes.

In *The Bruce Partington Plans*, the Metropolitan Railway is the setting for the murder of a man whose body was found along the underground tracks near Aldgate station. In his pocket were the top-secret plans for the Bruce-Partington Submarine. Holmes visits the scene of the crime to uncover clues. 'Is it a coincidence that it [the body] is found at the very point where the train pitches and sways as it comes round on the points?... Either the body fell from the roof, or a very curious coincidence has occurred. Now, suppose that a train halted under such a window, would there be any difficulty in laying a body upon the roof?... Owing to the intersection of one of the larger railways, the underground trains are frequently held motionless for some minutes at that very spot.' 'Splendid, Holmes! You have got it!' crooned the doggedly supportive Dr Watson, surely the greatest Sherlock Holmes fan ever.

In *The Final Problem*, Conan Doyle attempts to kill Holmes off with a spectacular plummet into the Reichenbach Falls in Switzerland, still grappling with his arch-enemy, the egregious Professor Moriarty. Before this piece of melodrama, he and Watson had caught a train from Victoria only to spot Moriarty on the platform vainly trying to get someone to stop the train. Moriarty had obviously tracked them down and this then caused Holmes and Watson to change their route plan.

They alighted at Canterbury and as they waited for another train, a special one-coach train roars past. It had, of course, been hired by Moriarty in an effort to overtake Holmes. The inseparable duo also travels from King's Cross station in *The Adventure of the Missing Three-Quarter* where Holmes suddenly exclaims that he has identified a starting point for their investigation. With that the engine whistles and the train plunges into the tunnel on the first part of its journey to Cambridge.

The proliferation of magazines and 'penny dreadfuls' (much criticised in the 1870s for being a bad influence on young working-class boys) with their lurid serialisations provided a plentiful supply of stories set around trains, stations and tunnels. Short stories about crime on the railway were abundant. Plots, rarely subtle, included bodies thrown from trains, innocent damsels (or sometimes dynamite) tied to the tracks, foreign spies and even double agents, cads who travel first class on third-class tickets, smugglers, saboteurs, and dead bodies (sometimes dismembered), turning up in trunks on stations or trains. On a number of occasions discussed elsewhere, this proved to be a case of life imitating art. Examples of the 'body-in-the-trunk' genre can be found in Henry Holt's *Murder on the Bookstall* (1934) which concerns the discovery of a woman's body at the bookstall on Charing Cross station and Agatha Christie's short story *The Plymouth Express* (1923), where a young naval officer on a train journey to Plymouth finds the dead body of a woman underneath one of the seats in his carriage.

Although most actual recorded crimes relating to the railways involved theft – either on a passenger train or by an employee stealing from the company – fictional narratives tended to look to more exciting and gruesome action. Night train stories feature especially in European journeys. Agatha Christie's *Murder on the Orient Express* (1934) typifies the glamour of such continental travel with its elaborate meals, rich and exotic passengers and romantic places. Sherlock Holmes, always ready to announce that 'the game is afoot', kept a copy of *Bradshaw's European Railway Timetable* on his mantelpiece. Nonetheless, Britain provided the setting for many of these overnight sleeper railway murders. In *The Mystery of the Sleeping Car Express* by Freeman Wills Crofts a murderer escapes from a moving train on the Euston to north Scotland line, while his victims and an innocent bystander are locked in their compartment.

Aldgate station opened in 1876. This is the northern end of the station with three steam-hauled trains visible. The drivers and firemen of the Metropolitan Railway locomotives needed to be made of stern stuff. The line into the tunnel on the left goes to Aldgate East.

Victor Lorenzo Whitechurch (1868-1933), a clergyman and author, wrote much detective fiction including *Thrilling Stories of the Railway* (1912). This collection contains fifteen stories, the first nine of which feature wealthy amateur investigator Thorpe Hazell, vegetarian and railway hobbyist. The stories vary from theft on the railways (e.g. *The Stolen Necklace* and *Sir Gilbert Murrell's Picture*), tobacco smuggling (*Peter Crane's Cigars*) to foreign spies masquerading as locomotive firemen. He also wrote stories for the *Strand Magazine* and *Railway Magazine* from the 1890s. Whitechurch's *Murder on the Okehampton Line*, which appeared in *Pearson's Magazine* in December 1903, opens with a newspaper report of a murder:

On the arrival of the last train from Exeter to Okehampton at the latter station last night, a gruesome discovery was made. A porter on the platform noticed a gentleman seated in the corner of a third class compartment and, as he made no attempt to get out of the carriage, opened the door to wake him, thinking he might be asleep. To his horror he discovered the man was dead and a subsequent examination revealed the fact that he been stabbed in the heart with some sharp instrument.

A modern view of Aldgate station frontage. This busy station in the City of London is currently used by trains on the Metropolitan and Circle lines.

As detective Godfrey Page investigates, his line of enquiry begins to resemble somewhat the Monty Python sketch ('Agatha Christie Timetable'):

> Let me see, the last down train arrives at Okehampton at ten-fifty. It's the one that leaves Waterloo at five-fifty and Exeter, St David's, at ten-thirty. Of course, the great question is where did he get into the train and whereabouts was he murdered?...These two men...could not have got away by train, for this was the last one at the junction that night...Number 242 third coach is one that is kept at Plymouth as a spare carriage in case there is an abnormal number of passengers for the Paddington express. The night to which you refer it ran – on the eight –twenty p.m. from North Road, Plymouth arriving here at 10.03.

What might seem to be nerdishly intimate knowledge of train timetables is crucial to getting the crime solved.

Murder is the theme of Miles Burton's *Death in the Tunnel* (1936) which features sleuths Desmond Merrion and Detective Inspector Arnold. They investigate the death of Sir Wilfred Saxonby who is discovered in a first-class carriage on the London to Stourford train. An eye-witness to a murder provides the opening to *4.50 from Paddington* (1957) by Agatha Christie. A passenger on a train, Elspeth McGillicuddy, who is traveling from Scotland, sees a woman strangled in a passing train. What has happened to the body? Who was the unfortunate victim? Who murdered her and why?

Thomas Hanshew (1857-1914) *The Riddle of the 5.28*. Written in 1910, this is one of the earliest stories to be set on the Brighton line from London. The train compartment becomes the scene of a gruesome discovery and the beginning of a deep and dark mystery. Typically where short stories are concerned there is no time to waste in getting to the point and Hanshew does this to good effect. A stationmaster at Anerley near Crystal Palace receives a communication: 'Five-twenty-eight down from London Bridge just passed. One first-class carriage compartment in total darkness. Investigate.' The porter and stationmaster do just that and find the said compartment with an 'Engaged' label on the window. As they unlock the door they make a dreadful discovery. 'For there in a corner, with his face towards the engine, half sat, half leaned the figure of a dead man with a bullet hole between his eyes.' What follows is an intriguing murder mystery, involving not only a whodunnit but also raising the question of how was it done given that 'both doors were locked and both window closed' when the body was discovered.

Travelling on the underground can be a risky enterprise when the threat of murderers and assassins looms. The London Underground, the first part of which commenced operations in 1863 and which now possesses over 250 miles of track and about 288 stations, has provided the setting for many novels and short stories. It is an ideal atmospheric setting for dark tales. *A Mystery of the Underground* (1897) by John Oxenham (1853-1941), was effective in scaring its readers when it was first published weekly in *To-Day*. The story concerns an assassin who is murdering people every Tuesday night on the underground. The tone is established right from the outset: 'The underground station at Charing Cross was the scene of considerable excitement on the night of Tuesday the fourth of November. As the 9.17 London & North Western train rumbled up the platform, a lady was standing at the door of one of the first-class carriages, frantically endeavouring to get out, and screaming wildly…she was in a state of violent hysterics.' Railway cognoscenti will raise their eyebrows at the idea of a London & North Western train being found at Charing Cross.

The presence of a dead body, sitting as though asleep, was the cause of the woman's desperate behaviour. As another body is discovered a week later at Ealing Broadway station, people are becoming reluctant to take the train. However, the murders do not deter the morbidly curious who crowd the platforms of Charing Cross, Westminster, St James and Victoria 'simply with the idea of being on the spot in case anything happens.' These 'throngs of

Cover of *Strand Magazine* which published most of the Sherlock Holmes stories in serial form.

people [wait] silently, in a damp fog, peering into carriage after carriage as the almost empty trains rolled slowly, like processions of funeral cars.' The body count adds up as they fall victim to the mysterious assassin's deadly bullets.

Baroness Emmuska Orczy's (1865-1947) 'The Mysterious Death on the Underground Railway' appeared as a short story in the book *The Old Man in the Corner* (1909). What appears to be the suicide of a woman in a carriage on the Metropolitan Railway turns out to be a murder. There is some similarity with the discovery of the body to that in *A Mystery of the Underground*. The guard 'noticed a lady sitting in the furthest corner, with her head turned away towards the window.' When the guard asks which station she wants the lady does not move, giving the impression that she is asleep. 'He touched her arm lightly and looked into her face…In the glassy eyes, the ashen colour of the cheeks, the rigidity of the head, there was the unmistakable look of death.'

The railway carriage proved to be an ideal setting for many situations other than murder such as theft, furtive and clandestine trysts between lovers, secret confabulations between spies and even sexual encounters, planned or entirely casual and spontaneous. Ian Carter quotes the interesting example of frequent quickies between stops: 'For a few years after 1866, services between Charing Cross and Cannon Street drew a curious traffic. Some ladies of the street had found that the South Eastern Railway's first-class compartments, combined with the uninterrupted seven-minute run, provided ideal conditions for their activities at a rental that represented only a minute proportion of their income.' The mind boggles.

As we saw with Sherlock Holmes, the carriage allows the possibility for reflection and even the working out of a murder. In Dorothy L. Sayers (1893-1957) *The Man with no Face* (1928) the discovery of a murdered man who had his 'face cut about in the most dreadful manner' on a beach at East Felpham becomes the topic of debate for passengers on a busy train who speculate about the foul deed. One of the passengers is Lord Peter Wimsey, the gentleman 'detective', who proceeds to solve the crime during the journey and beyond, just as you would expect.

Another example is in Agatha Christie's short story *The Girl in the Train* (1924) which features a dissolute playboy, George Rowland, who has taken a train from Waterloo to a place he spots in an ABC guide called *Rowland's Castle*. The journey changes his life dramatically when a beautiful girl bursts into his first-class compartment begging to be hidden from a villainous foreign man who then appears at the window and angrily demands that Rowland gives his niece back. The chivalrous George calls a platform guard who detains the man. The train departs and the adventure begins.

In Dinah Mulock Craik's (1826-1887) *A Life for a Life* (1859) a passenger notes the perils from drunks of travelling in a carriage late in the day:

I am liable to meet at least one drunken 'gentleman' snoozing in his first-class carriage; or, in second class, two or three drunken men, singing, swearing, or pushed stupidly about by pale-faced wives. The 'gentleman', often grey-haired, is but 'merry', as he is accustomed to be every night of his life; the poor man has only 'had a drop or two', as all his comrades are in the habit of taking, whenever they get the chance: they see no disgrace in it...It makes me sick at heart sometimes to see a decent, pretty girl sit tittering at a foul-mouthed beast opposite; or a tidy young mother, with two or three bonnie children, trying to coax home, without harm to himself or them, some brutish husband, who does not know his right hand from his left, so utterly stupid is he with drink.

A more eerie story is Basil Cooper's *The Second Passenger* (1973) where a man travels in an empty third-class carriage from Charing Cross and reflects on his past. The passenger is not all he seems in this macabre tale of a tall figure, green slime and a porter shouting 'what was it?'

The success of Britain's early railways inspired groups of businessmen to plan extensions to the rail system. Many did so with good intentions, others were no more than conmen and criminals. This latter group had no intention of building a railway, despite promises to investors who had lodged money with them. During the 1840s accusations of fraud and corruption abounded. Fraudulent and greedy railway speculators come under critical scrutiny in Anthony Trollope's (1815-1882) *The Way We Live Now* (1875). The central character, Augustus Melmotte, is a mysterious international financier described as a 'rich scoundrel... a bloated swindler... and a vile city ruffian' who desires to be accepted into the influential circles of Victorian society. He believes he has almost achieved this when he convinces a number of prominent London businessmen of a get-rich-quick scheme which turns out to be a corrupt corporation with the impressive name of the Great South Central Pacific & Mexican Railway. Among those convinced are the Carburys, an aristocratic but cash-strapped family desperate to recoup their fortunes by whatever means necessary.

In between the financial goings-on there are romances such as the one-sided romance between Melmotte's daughter Marie and the dissolute Sir Felix Carbury. The novel also includes the exploits of an American adventuress with a predilection for shooting her lovers. Melmotte manages to get himself accepted into high society as well as being elected as an MP on the strength of his dealings in railway stock which entail borrowing huge sums of money for other ambitious projects. Melmotte is eventually exposed by one of his creditors, Paul Montague, who does not wish to be a part of Melmotte's fraudulent deals. The railroad company's stock begins to plunge causing Melmotte's fortunes to sink as quickly as they rose. Meanwhile his angry creditors try to press for payment on their rapidly sinking investment.

What Trollope effectively does (and this has a contemporary ring) is to turn a critical eye not only on the aristocratic and middle class sections of society but also anyone who blindly worships money and aspires to have it. The sycophants who sucked up to Melmotte, like those who toadied to present-day financiers, get their fingers burnt. The aristocracy, in typically hypocritical fashion, was always happy to attend the parties at Melmotte's house and partake of his generous hospitality but now they spurn him. Shades of Hudson.

A comprehensive knowledge of railways was the defining mark of the stories written by Freeman Wills Crofts (1879-1957). Opinions differ over Crofts. Some consider him to be the doyen of British railway crime writing whilst others, less kindly, view his work as humdrum and plodding. For Crofts, attention to a well-constructed timetable could take precedence over human emotion, intrigue or evil cunning. Born in Dublin he worked in railway engineering and wrote detective stories as and when he could. His long series of novels, written between 1920 and 1957, feature his best-known character, Inspector French.

Writing in what is often regarded as the 'Golden Age of Crime Fiction', which was the 1920s to the 1940s, his books included *The Cask* (1920), *The Sea Mystery* (1928), *The 12:30 from Croydon* (1934), *Death of a Train* (1946) and *Mystery of the Sleeping Car Express: And Other Stories* (1956). In *Inspector French's Greatest Case* (1925), a clerk of a diamond merchant firm is found murdered and the safe plundered. Inspector French painstakingly analyses railway timetables (his specialism) as part of his attempt to track the suspects. In many of his books, Crofts demonstrates a detailed knowledge of the railway network and its complexities, as if he enjoys showing off this knowledge and perhaps when it is not always germane to the plot.

In *Crime on the Footplate* (1955) Crofts starts in his trademark style: 'The August day was stifling as the 11.55a.m. express from Leeds beat heavily up the grade towards the summit in the foothills of the Pennines. From there the run down to Carlisle would be easy and rapid. The train was on time and travelling at the full thirty miles an hour customary at the place... All seemed well with the train, yet all was not well.' All was not well indeed, because on the footplate Fireman Grover was planning to murder his driver, William Deane.

Railway tunnels feature as crime scenes in many narratives. In the short story *The Mystery of the Felwyn Tunnel* (1898) by L.T. (Elizabeth Thomasina) Meade (1854-1914), Robert Eustace, a signalman has been found dead at the mouth of a tunnel in suspicious circumstances. Shortly after another signalman is also discovered dead in the same place. The Lytton Vale Railway Company in Wales calls in a detective to solve the mystery and the investigation begins.

Railway tracks are the setting for the discovery of a horribly mangled body that appears to have been dragged along by a train in *Dead on the Track* (1943),

Anthony Trollope (1815-82) achieved success with his 'Barchester' novels with their effective plots and characterisation. He used trains extensively during his time as a Post Office Surveyor. In that role, he was responsible for the erection of some of the earliest postal pillar boxes; in this case in the Channel Islands.

by John Rhode. In another story by Rhode, *Death on the Boat Train* (1940), Waterloo station is the site where a dead body is found following the arrival of the Southampton boat train. Another variation on the railway station is Margery Allingham's *Dancers in Mourning* (1937) where a bomb planted at a station blows up a murder suspect. Ethel Lina White's (1876-1944) short story, *Cheese* (1941), which appears in Peter Haining's collection *Murder on the Railways* (1996), sees Victoria station as the location for a tale of murder. Interestingly, Alfred Hitchcock's classic film *The Lady Vanishes* (1938) is based on the novel *The Wheel Spins* (1936) by White.

Train crashes are not always what they seem. A suspicious accident involving a steam engine and an electric train is the theme in *The Knight's Cross Signal Problem* (*News of the World* 24-31 August 1913) by Ernest Bramah. 'An ordinary Central and Suburban passenger train, travelling non-stop at Knight's Cross, ran past the signal and crashed into a crowded electric train that was just beginning to move out... For the first time on an English railway there was a good stand-up smash between a heavy steam engine and a train of light cars... Twenty-seven killed, forty something injured, eight died since... But was the engine-driver responsible?'

No doubt if most people were asked to name a story involving both railways and crime they would probably say *Thirty-Nine Steps* (1915) by John

Buchan which has also been adapted into a number of film versions. The novel, which introduces the famous adventuring hero, Richard Hannay, is set in 1914. Hannay hears of a plot to destabilise Europe beginning with a plan to assassinate the Greek Premier. Our hero is soon fleeing from German spies. Hannay decides to go to Scotland and a 'search in Bradshaw informed [him] that a train left St Pancras at 7.10' and would arrive at any Galloway station in the late afternoon. As the train progressed through Scotland, it 'rumbled slowly into a land of little wooded glens and then to a great wide moorland place, gleaming with lochs, with high blue hills showing northwards.' The film has a different take on the railway journey but more of that later.

More recent books about railway crime include those by Andrew Martin and there is no ambiguity about the subject of his books with titles such as *The Necropolis Railway* (2002), *The Lost Luggage Porter* (2006), *Murder at Deviation Point* (2007), *Death on a Branch Line* (2008), and *The Last Train to Scarborough* (2009). The first of these, *The Necropolis Railway,* is set against the engine sheds around Nine Elms, Waterloo and the eponymous Necropolis Railway at Brookwood at the turn of the nineteenth century. The central character is Jim Stringer who starts his career on the railways only to find that his predecessors have met a premature and gruesome end. It seems that Stringer might become the next victim.

Edward Marston is another contemporary writer who has written some forty crime novels. His series about the railways involves the dandy Robert Colbeck, an Inspector in the Detective Department of the Metropolitan Police in the nineteenth century. Marston's books include *The Railway Detective, The Excursion Train, The Railway Viaduct, The Iron Horse* and *Murder on the Brighton Express. The Railway Detective* is set in 1851 where the London to Birmingham mail train is stopped and derailed, seriously injuring the driver. Colbeck is faced with solving the well-organised train robbery.

In *Underground* (2000) by Tobias Hill, a mysterious person is pushing women under trains, and a Polish immigrant who works at a north London station – a loner with a complicated past and a secret fear of the dark – is determined to stop the killings.

These, and other, contemporary writers continue a tradition as old as the railways and by so doing reflect an ongoing interest and enthusiasm for those particular areas that still carry a fascination: railways, crime and reading.

The entrance to the former Necropolis Railway part of Waterloo station. The Necropolis Railway opened in 1854 connecting Waterloo with Brookwood cemetery near Woking. Much of this part of the station was destroyed by enemy action in the Second World War.

RAILWAY CRIME ON THE SCREEN

John Huntly aptly makes the point in his book, *Railways and the Cinema* (1969) that 'like the steam locomotive, there is no exact moment in time when the cinema came into existence.' Whenever that moment was, film-makers quickly tapped into the potential of railways as an ideal subject for films. Starting with a range of silent documentaries such as *Express Trains* (1898), *Railway Ride Over the Tay Bridge* (1897) and *Building a British Railway* (1905), feature films soon followed. Typically it was the United States that responded to this with films such as *The Great Train Robbery* (1903), *The Lost Freight Car* (1911) and *Helen's Sacrifice* (1914).

British film-makers followed with *When the Devil Drives* (1907), a rather surreal film, in which a taxi driver of a four-wheeled cab takes a suburban family to a railway station. Suddenly the cab driver changes into the Devil. As he arrives at the station he then mysteriously vanishes, leaving the confused passengers alone with their luggage. As they board the train and settle down the Devil reappears, this time as the train driver. The Devil gets rid of the driver and his mate and then embarks on an incredible journey, much to the anguish of the terrified passengers. The film ends with a close-up of the Devil's manic, laughing face. Following the success of American serials such as *The Hazards of Helen*, British attempts at the genre included *Lieutenant Daring and the Plans of the Minefields* (1913), which involved villains travelling by train from Charing Cross to Folkstone.

Towards the end of the silent era *The Wrecker* (1929) was adapted into film by Gainsborough from a stage play written by Arnold Ridley. The story concerns an engine driver who believes his engine is malevolent. His fears are confirmed in the finale when there is a huge train crash. Arnold Ridley

(1896–1984), probably more well known for his role as Private Charles Godfrey in *Dad's Army* which ran on television from 1968 to 1977, also wrote *The Ghost Train* (1923) which was a huge success for over two years when performed at St Martin's theatre in London. It was later adapted into a film, first in 1931 with the comedian Jack Hulbert and the better known version in 1941 starring Arthur Askey. Ridley's inspiration for writing the play came from stories he had heard about Mangotsfield station in Bristol, closed in 1962. The 1931 version made generous use of the Great Western Railway with a number of scenic shots en route from Paddington.

The *Ghost Train* centres on a group of passengers travelling to Cornwall who miss their connection and have to spend the night in the waiting room of a remote and eerie railway station called Fal Vale. While they wait, an agitated stationmaster tries to persuade them to leave because, he warns them, there is a local legend of a ghost train that brings doom and death to all who see it. During the night the stationmaster is murdered and tensions begin to mount. However, as we discover later, the train is in fact smuggling arms and the story has been concocted to frighten away strangers.

Gainsborough also made the 1941 remake of *The Ghost Train*. This film was made at the Lime Grove studios because railway stations were unavailable for filming during the war. The film was shot in several locations around Devon and Cornwall. In addition to Askey (who plays Tommy Gander, a concert comedian) it included his straight-man Richard 'Stinker' Murdoch (1907–1990) who played Teddy Deakin. Many would regard Arthur Askey's inane antics as spoiling what is otherwise a good film.

Although the sound film appeared in Britain in 1928, there were still long periods of silent footage. *The Flying Scotsman* (1930) which starred Ray Milland was such an example, and for the first half-hour it was silent. In the film an elderly engine driver, who is due to retire the following day, reports a fireman for drunkenness. The angry fireman sets out to get revenge by striking the driver on what is his last journey. The daughter of the driver comes to the rescue by taking over the train and bringing it to an eventual standstill. Despite some unfavourable reviews the film endeared itself to railway enthusiasts by depicting many scenes showing locomotives and trains of the London & North Eastern Railway.

More interestingly, according to John Huntley, the director Castleton Knight managed to make use of Gresley Pacific No.4472 *Flying Scotsman* for ten Sunday mornings from King's Cross to Edinburgh. In the 1933 film *Friday the Thirteenth* (nothing to do with the 'slasher' series of films) with Jessie Matthews and comedian Max Miller, King's Cross station is used as the location in which to introduce two of the main characters.

The Silent Passenger (1935) was the first adaptation of a Dorothy L. Sayer's story involving Lord Peter Wimsey (played by Peter Haddon). The story, which

Flying Scotsman at Doncaster resplendent in London & North Eastern Railway apple green livery. Opinion continues to be divided about the aesthetic effect of the later modifications with the German-style smoke deflectors and the double chimney. This is arguably the world's most famous steam locomotive.

was written specifically for the screen, involves a scurrilous blackmailer who is murdered by the husband of one of his victims, railroad detective Henry Camberley (Henry Wolfit). However, it is the innocent John Ryder (John Loder) who is suspected of the crime when Camberley stuffs the dead body into his trunk. Wimsey sets about to prove his new friend's innocence and the action takes place on a train trip from London to the English Channel.

Kate Plus Ten (1937), which features some lively sequences of trains at speed, is a light-hearted comedy based on an Edgar Wallace novel written in 1917. The eponymous Kate Westhanger (Genevieve Tobin) is the leader of a gang of crooks as well as secretary to Lord Flamborough. Kate and her gang are planning to rob Flamborough's £600,000 gold bullion shipment which is on a train between Seahampton and London (the scenes were filmed in and around

Bath). Scotland Yard Inspector Mike Pemberton (Jack Hulbert) is onto Kate's scheme and unbeknown to Kate the gang members are double-crossing her. As the bullion arrives at Seahampton docks the thieves uncouple the carriage and make off with the bullion on a runaway train. Kate and Inspector Pemberton board a locomotive in an attempt to cut off the gang's getaway cars.

Another film dealing with car and train chases and starring Jack Hulbert again in the pursuit of thieves is *Bulldog Jack* (1935). Captain Hugh 'Bulldog' Drummond (Atholl Fleming) is injured when his sabotaged car is involved in a crash, and so Jack Pennington (Hulbert), a first-class cricketer, agrees to impersonate Drummond in order to help the heroine, Ann Manders (Fay Wray). She needs to find her jeweller grandfather who has been kidnapped by a gang of crooks who want him to copy a valuable necklace which they intend to steal. Their plan backfires in the British Museum and the film climaxes in an exciting chase on a runaway train in the London Underground. The interesting railway part of the film includes a number of scenes shot at the disused British Museum tube station which was closed in 1933.

Seven Sisters (1936) moves from Nice and Paris to Hampshire and includes a murder, three train crashes and a gunfight. *The Last Journey* (1936) like *The Flying Scotsman*, features an engine driver making his last journey. However, in this film the driver, finding it difficult to come to terms with his retirement and dwelling on his domestic problems, drives his train at breakneck speed, ignoring all signals. As the passengers become increasingly fearful they all wish they knew how to stop the train. The passengers include two petty criminals, a crook in a bigamous marriage and a detective in disguise. The Great Western Railway gave full co-operation to the film company, allowing them extensive use of track and signal boxes, trains and coaches as well as providing materials and technical advice.

In 1937 the comedy classic, *Oh Mr Porter*, was released starring Will Hay (1888-1949) in his best-known role as the new stationmaster, William Porter, of a remote and highly rustic Northern Ireland railway station at Buggleskelly, not far from the border with the Republic. Together with his fellow workers, played by Moore Marriott as Jeremiah Harbottle and Graham Moffatt as Albert, they encounter the legend of 'One-Eyed Joe' a ghost who is said to haunt the lonely station. The local postman (Dave O'Toole) takes great pleasure in telling the legend to the new stationmaster: 'Every night when the moon gives light, The ghost of the miller is seen, As he walks the track with a sack on his back, Down to the Black Borheen... He haunts the station, he haunts the hill, And the land that lies between.'

The legend, as with many other local legends, turns out to be a distraction used by gun-runners to conceal their criminal activities. This was a real tactic used in coastal villages when tales of ghosts coming out at night provided a means of keeping people off the street whilst smugglers went about their business. Filmed mainly around the abandoned Basingstoke–Alton branch line of the Southern Railway, the film was summed up by one review which commented on its timeless quality, 'set in a poetic limbo, where nothing will ever change.'

The 1931 bestselling novel by A.J. Cronin, *Hatter's Castle* (1933), was loosely adapted as a film in 1941. Made by Paramount Pictures it had a star cast which included Robert Newton, Deborah Kerr and James Mason. The story, set in the year 1879, is a bleak drama about the ruin that befalls a Scottish hatter (Newton), a social climber set on recapturing his imagined lost nobility. He lives in a castle-like residence nicknamed Hatter's Castle and rules his family like a tyrant. His timid daughter, Mary (Kerr), is seduced, becomes pregnant and is thrown out of her home. The scene most pertinent to the railway is the one in which Mary leaves the train carriage to wander off into the darkness.

The decision is one that saves Mary's life as the Tay Bridge collapses during a gale force wind with the train and all its passengers (including Dennis, played by Emlyn Wiliams, the man who seduced her), plunging to their deaths. More misery follows with bankruptcy for the hatter, Brodie. His son commits suicide after he is caught cheating in an exam and Brodie burns down his palatial home destroying himself along with it. It is believed that *Hatter's Castle* is the only film that depicts the Tay Bridge disaster.

Waterloo Road (1944) is a Gainsborough picture starring John Mills, Stewart Granger and Alastair Sim. It is mainly concerned with life in wartime Britain and focuses on the problems faced by a number of different families in such difficult times. Although railway relevance is rather thin it does include a chase across the tracks outside Waterloo station. A very dangerous thing to do in view of the electric conductor rails.

Those familiar with the Basil Rathbone (Holmes) and Nigel Bruce (Watson) series of films about Sherlock Holmes will know they bear only the most tenuous connection to the Conan Doyle stories. In these films Holmes is variously fighting the Nazis or flying off to Washington. Nonetheless they proved enormously popular and established Rathbone, much to his regret, in the forefront of the pantheon of actors who have played Holmes. The film *Terror by Night* (1946) made by Universal Pictures in the USA is set almost entirely on an overnight train travelling from London to Edinburgh.

Accompanied by Dr Watson and Inspector Lestrade (Dennis Hoey), Holmes has been hired to prevent the theft of the Star of Rhodesia, an enormous 400-plus carat diamond owned by Lady Margaret Carstairs (Mary Forbes). As Holmes switches diamonds with Lady Margaret, her son Roland (Geoffrey Steele) is murdered shortly after and the fake diamond is stolen. Holmes believes that the notorious criminal Colonel Sebastian Moran (Professor Moriarty's henchman) is involved in the murder and the theft.

This is all that can now be seen of Cliddesden station on the highly rustic and long-closed Basingstoke to Alton railway line. This rather pointless line was built by the London & South Western Railway and it was immortalised by playing a central role in the film 'Oh, Mr Porter'.

Plenty of action takes place on the train and in addition to the murder of Roland Carstairs, Holmes and Watson unearth in the luggage compartment a train guard murdered by a tiny poisonous dart made out of a fiendishly clever dissolving substance.

Filmed in black and white, *Terror by Night* creates a good atmosphere despite several gaffs, including some of the exterior shots of the train. These show trains of different companies and also include a model and some foreign trains. Enthusiasts will know that such faux pas are by no means unusual in films showing moving trains. As the film was made in 1946 the studio did not find it necessary to use the wartime propaganda prevalent in some of the earlier films.

After the war, restrictions on filming did not suffer from the same limitations but there had also been significant changes to the railway industry. The Labour government had a mandate to nationalise the railways and the Transport Act was passed in 1947. The railways were nationalised on 1 January 1948. The Act brought virtually all railways, including London Underground, under the control of the British Transport Commission (BTC) although the name British Railways came into immediate use for day-to-day purposes.

In *Train of Events* (1949) the London, Midland & Scottish Railway, which was absorbed into British Railways during the making of the film, provided the main locations around Willesden and Euston. The film offers a slight variation on the crashed train theme by attempting, not very successfully, to follow the stories of three sets of people as they travel on a night train from Euston to Liverpool. Although not specifically a ghost story, there is a sense of impending doom underpinning the tale.

The engine driver, played by Jack Warner, says what will be a tragic and inevitable farewell to his wife. The passengers include an actor who has murdered his unfaithful wife, an orphan girl who is in love with a fugitive German prisoner of war, and a famous conductor who cannot choose between his wife and a glamorous pianist. Although the doomed train will cruelly resolve the problems of the characters, the audience is left to speculate on who will survive.

During the 1950s British cinema went through a number of important changes as audiences fell and many cinemas closed down (as did railway stations). Many critics (not entirely correctly) viewed the decline in attendance as being accompanied by a decline in the standard of films. British films came to be seen as dull and conservative. The war film was popular (for example, *The Cruel Sea* (1953), *The Dam Busters* (1955), *Reach for the Sky* (1956), *The Bridge on the River Kwai* (1957)) as were comedy films, notably those coming out of Ealing Studios (*The Lavender Hill Mob* (1951), and *The Ladykillers* (1955)). Ealing Studios are the oldest working film studios in the world, dating back over a century, and Ealing films became synonymous with genteel British comedy.

The Ladykillers (1955) is a dark comedy starring Alec Guinness, Peter Sellers, Herbert Lom and Jack Warner. 'Professor' Marcus (Guinness) rents rooms for a diverse gang of oddball criminals in a ramshackle house not far from King's Cross, owned by an eccentric octogenarian widow, Mrs Louisa Wilberforce (Katie Johnson) who lives alone except for her parrots. The intention of the gang is to rob a security van at King's Cross station. Meanwhile the Professor convinces Mrs Wilberforce that they are amateur musicians who want the room to rehearse, hence they carry instruments and play a recording of Boccherini's Minuet, appropriately a string quintet, while they plan their heist.

Once they have completed their successful robbery they deposit the money in the station parcel office. Mrs Wilberforce stumbles on the truth when on leaving her house one of the gang manages to trap his cello case in the door allowing all the banknotes to flutter out. Fearing that she will tell the police, the gang decides it has no option but to get rid of her. However, no one actually wants to do it. They soon fall out and begin to kill each other with the bodies being dropped into railway wagons. In the end they are all dead and dear old Mrs Wilberforce is left holding the money.

Mrs Wilberforce's 'lopsided' house was a set built at the western end of Frederica Street, directly above the southern portal of Copenhagen Tunnel on the railway line leading out of King's Cross station. The film used a number of locations around King's Cross including Copenhagen Tunnel; Cheney Road, St Pancras (the scene of the robbery); the North London Line; York Way;

the famous King's Cross Gasholders and various roads around Islington and Holloway. This film is a great favourite with railway enthusiasts because of its footage of steam trains working in and out of King's Cross.

Four years previous to *The Lady Killers*, *Mystery Junction* (1951) was released. It follows a rather complicated plot with a crime novelist concocting a story about fellow passengers on the train for the benefit of a young woman. On the train is a prisoner who is being taken to court as a suspect in a murder case. The passengers are told by the policeman escorting him to disembark at a lonely snowbound station so that everybody can be interviewed while they wait for the police to arrive. As this is happening the lights go out and one of the prisoner's accomplices cuts the phone line. Shots are fired and the policeman lies dead on the floor, suspicion falling on one of the passengers.

Murder and/or robbery have been the main staple for railway crime films. Robbery is very much the theme of *The Flying Scot* (1957). Travelling overnight on the *Flying Scotsman*, a group of robbers start to make a large hole between two compartments in order to gain access to sacks of money. When a young boy finds out what is happening, he informs the guard who throws a written message out of the window to a signalman telling him to call the police. The robbers are eventually arrested.

Ten years later came *Robbery* (1967) which was loosely based on the Great Train Robbery of 1963. With only the passing of four years the 1963 robbery was still fresh in the minds of the public and there was still some sensitivity which was evident in the use of twenty lawyers to ensure there was no possibility of libel against the film company. Starring Stanley Baker, James Booth and Frank Finlay, the film opens with a jewel robbery which is intended to fund a bigger, better organised robbery of the overnight mail train from Glasgow to London. The 12.30 night express is successfully held up and the gang members escape to an unused airfield to share out the £2.6 million. However, one of the robbers had foolishly called his wife from a phone box during the raid and the police had tapped his house phone. With one exception the robbers are all eventually arrested. One of the locations for the film was Husbands Bosworth near Market Harborough. The train robbery had a huge media coverage which provided a convenient distraction for the Conservative Government of the day who were deeply embarrassed at the time by the Profumo scandal.

The controversial Beeching report, produced while Richard Beeching was chairman of British Railways between 1963 and 1965, attempted to reduce the losses being sustained by the national railway system. It advocated widespread closures. In the event, more than 4,000 miles of railway and 3,000 stations closed in the decade following the report. The scrapping of a village station (and a nod to the Great Train Robbery) is the topical subject of the children's film made in 1965, *Runaway Railway*. Barming station (Borden) has been targeted by Government cuts and its steam engine, *Matilda*, has to be scrapped. It is down to four children to try and run the line as a private concern with the help of local landowner, Lord Chalk.

As a Government official visits the village, the children try to buy time by sabotaging the train. In order to raise money for repairs a fund-raising dance for local children is held at the station. Lurking around the station are two dodgy-looking men claiming to be train enthusiasts but their real intent is to rob a London-bound mail van. In true fantasy style the children foil the robbery by driving *Matilda*, the lovable little steam engine. They receive a reward which goes towards saving the private line. It is almost reminiscent of an Ealing film, where the small rural community defeats not only the robbers but also chases the Government official (in standard pinstripe and umbrella) out of the village.

A train robbery from an earlier period, the Great South Eastern Train Robbery is the subject of *The First Great Train Robbery* (1978) starring Sean Connery and Donald Sutherland. Michael Crichton, who based it on his bestselling thriller, directed the film. Although set in London and Kent, most of the filming was done in Ireland. The original robbery took place in May 1855 when three London firms sent a box of gold bars and coins from London Bridge to Paris via the South Eastern Railway. The gold was stolen en route.

The story is loosely based on this robbery, in which Edward Pierce (Connery) is a master thief with the goal of stealing a shipment of gold bars en route to the Crimea. With the help of England's greatest locksmith, Agar (Donald Sutherland), Pierce sets out to copy each of four keys needed to open the train's vault, keys that are kept and guarded by different parties. The robbery was filmed on a vintage passenger train in which Pierce clambers along the entire length of the fast-moving train, leaping from carriage to carriage and ducking under low bridges.

1978 saw the third film adaptation of John Buchan's *The Thirty-Nine Steps* (1935, 1959, 1978). In the 1935 version, which starred Robert Donat and Madelaine Carroll and was directed by Alfred Hitchcock, Richard Hannay is a Canadian visitor to London who goes to a music hall and sees 'Mr Memory's' show, where he meets Annabella Smith who is trying to escape from secret agents. Hannay helps by hiding her in his flat where she claims to have uncovered a plot to steal vital British military secrets. She mentions the 'thirty-nine steps', but does not explain its meaning and the mystery further deepens when she is murdered by a mystery intruder during the night, using Hannay's breadknife.

Now a key suspect, he goes on the run to break the spy ring. He takes a train to Scotland (because she had told him she was going to visit a man there), and as the police search the train in desperation, he enters a compartment and kisses the one person in it (Carroll), as a distraction. Still pursued,

Hannay jumps from the train onto the Forth Rail Bridge and escapes. Hannay makes his way through parts of Scotland until he reaches his destination only to find that the occupant, the seemingly respectable Professor Jordan, is part of the spy ring. Hannay is eventually captured and handcuffed but he realises that the policemen are part of the conspiracy. Our hero escapes yet again and drags an unwilling Madelaine Carroll (Pamela) along.

The story concludes back in London at 'Mr Memory's' show. The spies are cunningly using Mr Memory to smuggle the secrets out. Hannay asks 'Mr Memory', 'What are the thirty-nine steps?' to which he replies, 'it is an organisation of spies, collecting information on behalf of the foreign office…' The unfortunate Mr Memory is shot, but before he dies he tells of a design for a silent aircraft engine. The film does not stick to Buchan's novel. There is a love interest in the film, and in the book the thirty-nine steps refer to physical steps (as do other film versions).

The 1959 version is very much a product of the 1950s with an array of almost comic characters. It still uses the Forth Bridge but the film does not match either the 1935 or the 1978 adaptation. In the latter, Robert Powell plays Hannay and the film adheres more faithfully to the book. Set in early 1914, before the onset of war, Colonel Scudder (John Mills), a retired British Intelligence Service agent has discovered a plot to assassinate the Greek Prime Minister on a visit to London. Hannay goes to the scene of Scudder's murder at St Pancras station and discovers his much-thumbed notebook, full of vital information. Thereafter follows a series of escapes across the country, with both foreign agents and the police on Hannay's trail.

Following the end of steam on British Railways in 1968, nostalgia became something of an industry, with steam appearing in a number of films including *The Railway Children* (1970) and Agatha Christie's *Murder on the Orient Express* (1974). In a different type of remembrance, the twenty-fifth anniversary of the Great Train Robbery of 1963 was reflected in a film about one of the junior robbers. The robbery had made celebrities of some of the criminals, who raided the Glasgow to London mail train and made off with £2.6m in used bank notes on 8 August 1963.

Buster (1988) tells the story of Buster Edwards played by Phil Collins. Opinions are divided over the train robbers. The fact that the fifteen men managed to plan the robbery in a very careful and meticulous way and steal £2.6 million contrasts with the bungling whereby they got themselves arrested and imprisoned. *Buster* projected itself as a romantic thriller, placing more emphasis on Edward's relationship with his family than on the robbery itself. He and his family go into hiding before finally heading for Mexico. However, the money soon dries up and his wife (played by Julie Walters) misses her family, so Edwards decides to return to England and give himself up. Billed as a romantic thriller, *Buster* falls short of thrills and does not match up to *Robbery* (1967). The locations used in *Buster* included Loughborough and Rothley stations on the Great Central Railway in Leicestershire.

Paddington station makes a brief appearance in the British gangster film *The Long Good Friday* (1980) when Carol Benson (Patti Love) collects the body of her husband, murdered in Northern Ireland, while doing a spot of work for Jeff Hughes. The station was also featured in the murder mystery *The October Man* (1947) with John Mills and Joan Greenwood.

The London Underground has featured in numerous short stories and novels as well as many films and TV productions. Not all have been about crime, possibly because of the difficulties in sustaining a full-length story set on the underground that deals with crime. Horror or supernatural films, although only a few have been made, have featured better, such as *Quatermass and the Pit* (1967), *Death Line* (1972) and *Creep* (2004).

Earlier films such as Roman Polanski's *Repulsion* (1965), a study of a murderous psychopath, features South Kensington station. However, more recent films that include scenes on the underground are *The Fourth Protocol* (1987), which features a double agent being followed on the Piccadilly line between Hyde Park Corner and Green Park, although it was actually shot on the Jubilee line between Charing Cross and Green Park. There is also a scene in the film at Aldwych where Michael Caine takes his vengeance out on two racist yobs.

Also at Aldwych was *The Good Shepherd* (2006), a spy film starring Matt Damon and Angelina Jolie. *Die Another Day* (2002) is a James Bond film with Pierce Brosnan. Bond enters a small building on the south side of Westminster Bridge and descends to the disused 'Vauxhall Cross' station to meet 'M' (Judi Dench). In *Patriot Games* (1992) an IRA agent is chased from his bookshop on Charing Cross Road to a Piccadilly line station which is supposed to sound like Aldwych. There are some dreadful errors concerning the underground system in this film. *Green Street Hooligans* (2005), also known as *Hooligans*, is about a young American student (Elijah Wood) who moves to London and is introduced to drinking and football violence. Locations include Bank and East Finchley stations. *The Krays* (1990) has a scene of the Blitz where Aldwych is used for Bethnal Green, and *Killing Me Softly* (2002) features Canary Wharf.

A number of films have been made in the past two decades that have involved railway crime as the main setting for the plot, although most of these have either been made or set in countries other than Britain: *Money Train* (US 1995), *Death Train* (US 1993), *The Burning Train* (India 2000) and *The Taking of Pelham 123* (US 2009 remake of the 1974 classic). Although trains are used as a backcloth, few British films or films set in Britain have taken the railways as the main location, but *Mona Lisa* (1986) uses Liverpool Street station.

The excellent *Navigators* (2001), directed by Ken Loach, was a timely reflection on the effects of privatisation of the railway. It drew on the experiences of Rob Dawber, a railway man of seventeen years, who sadly died while the film was being made. Filmed at Loughborough and Sheffield the film is set during the 1980s when British Rail was being privatised. It follows the fortunes of a gang of workers who are faced with unpalatable changes brought on by corporate desire to maximise profits in every way possible.

The crime that Loach deals with is that of corporate negligence. As the film unfolds the gang of men is made redundant but return to employment as contractors with earnings that, on the surface, look attractive. However, their jobs are only short-term and without such benefits as holiday or sick pay. Workers are now, in corporate speak, a 'flexible' labour force with flexibility only working one way. Those who have a history of union involvement are blacklisted by agencies. The film begins with the men laughing at the banal transparency of mission statements and 'quality' procedures (which have very little to do with real quality) and being addressed by the foreman who is trying to be serious:

'Now listen, this really is important: Deaths must be kept to an acceptable level.'

'What's 'an acceptable level?'

'Er, two a year.'

'But nobody's been killed for the past eighteen months.'

This opening banter is important because behind the pretence of the marketing image, (reflected in the regular change of name and logo), the company, in its drive to maximise profits, cuts corners by reducing the number of workers and this results in the death of one of them at the end. The film offers a strong statement about changes to the railways in the late twentieth century in that the tragedy that occurs is a direct result of political decisions based on the dogma of the free market.

Particular mention should be given to *The Bourne Ultimatum* (2007) for its use of Waterloo station. This was the third Bourne film and was based loosely on Robert Ludlum's novel. Starring Matt Damon, Albert Finney and Joan Allen the story is about the amnesiac Jason Bourne (Damon) who used to work for the elite Special Activities Division. However, in his attempt to discover his real identity CIA assassins are pursuing him. As he flees from country to country the English action begins when Simon Ross (Paddy Considine), security correspondent from *The Guardian*, receives leaks from a CIA bureau chief. Bourne reads his name in a newspaper article and attempts to reach Ross before CIA operative Paz (Édgar Ramírez) catches up with him.

Bourne and Ross arrange to meet at the south entrance of Waterloo station, but the CIA has managed to track Bourne and it monitors the pair on the station's surveillance system. Bourne discovers that CIA agents are at the station. He then instructs Ross by mobile phone how to dodge the surveillance cameras. Paz, armed with a small assault rifle, pursues Bourne and Ross through the station onto York Road. The journalist panics and steps out into the open, thus allowing one of the assassins to shoot him. The dead Ross has information on him that Bourne needs and in the ensuing chaos Bourne grabs the notes and discovers more about the plot to kill him. The cat-and-mouse chase (which was filmed among real commuters) and eventual shoot-out at Waterloo station is impressive. The British Transport Police assisted the shooting scenes and the feeds from Waterloo's security cameras were used. Clearly much careful planning had gone into filming this particular action scene. In addition to Waterloo station the platform at Charing Cross underground station was used for the film.

Waterloo station has also been the location for *Incendiary* (2008) which portrays the aftermath of a terrorist attack at a football match starring Ewan McGregor and Matthew Macfadyen; *London to Brighton* (2006), a gritty British film that deals with violent mobsters and underage sex-slave trade; *Breaking and Entering* (2006) with Jude Law; *Outlaw* (2007) with Sean Bean and Bob Hoskins, about a group of men who feel let down by the law and decide to become vigilantes. Many TV productions have also been filmed there. It is a grand and imposing station and its possibilities have clearly been appreciated by generations of film-makers.

Shadows in the Steam
The Haunted Railways of Britain
David Brandon & Alan Brooke

Ghosts traditionally make their presence felt in many ways, from unexplained footfalls and chills to odours and apparitions. This fascinating volume takes a look at some of the strange and unexplained hauntings across Britain's railway network: signals and messages sent from empty boxes; trains that went into tunnels and never left; ghostly passengers and spectral crew; the wires whizzing to signal the arrival of trains on lines that have been closed for years.... Based on hundreds of first-person and historical accounts, *Shadows in the Steam* is a unique collection of mysterious happenings, inexplicable events and spine-chilling tales, all related to the railways.

978 0 7524 5224 1

The destination for history
www.thehistorypress.co.uk